THE GIVE TO GET PRINCIPLE

HOW RELATIONSHIPS & RECIPROCITY BUILD RAVING FANS

BY JENNIFER FILZEN

FOREWORD BY CARMAN CAPRIOTTO

JENNIFERFILZEN.COM

DEDICATION

To Mother and Daddy.
I first learned about reciprocity
from watching your journey
together in business.
Thank you for teaching me
how to be successful.
Rest In Peace, Daddy.

The Give To Get Principle: How Relationships & Reciprocity Build Raving Fans

Copyright © 2020 Jennifer Filzen.

All Rights Reserved.

With the exception of short reviews, no part of this book may be reproduced, stored in a retrieval system, or transmitted in any other form, or by any other means, electronic, mechanical, photocopying, recording, computer networking, or by any other means without prior permission in writing from Jennifer Filzen.

Printed in the U.S.A.
Book design by Rene Arreola

First Edition - December 2020

TABLE OF CONTENTS

CHAPTER 1   Introduction 3

CHAPTER 2   Successful Strategies Of The Top Shops 7

CHAPTER 3   Knowing Your Why 13

CHAPTER 4   Building Self Confidence 17

CHAPTER 5   The Four Currencies 23

CHAPTER 6   The Difference Between You & The Top 10%... 31

CHAPTER 7   Whys + Superpowers + Attitude = Raving Fans... 37

CHAPTER 8   Penguins & Auto Repair Shops 51

CHAPTER 9   Giving & Relationship Marketing 61

CHAPTER 10   We All Scream For Ice Cream 67

CHAPTER 11   The COVID Effect 71

CHAPTER 12   Thriving Beyond Surviving 75

CHAPTER 13   Together, We Are Stronger 77

CHAPTER 14
Action Step #1 – Start By Finding Your Why 83

CHAPTER 15
Action Step #2 – Discover The Superpower Of Yourself And Your Team 89

CHAPTER 16
Action Step #3 – Pay Attention To Attitude 93

CHAPTER 17
Action Step #4 – Define What You're Willing To Give To Get 99

CHAPTER 18
Action Step #5 – Examples Of The Giveaways Other Businesses Use 103

CHAPTER 19
Action Step #6 – Decide What You Can Give Freely Right Now...... 107

CHAPTER 20
Action Step #7 – Involve Your Team In Giving To Get 111

CHAPTER 21
Action Step #8 – Track And Measure Your Progress................ 115

Chapter 22
Action Step #9 – Building Community...................................... 117

CHAPTER 23
Action Step #10 – Mentor Others In Abundance Mentality.......... 121

CHAPTER 24
Action Step #11 – Ideas For Other Industries 125

CHAPTER 25 Are You Willing? 137

Foreword by Carman Capriotto

Five years ago, I started this extraordinary journey in helping automotive service professionals share their success journey through storytelling. I realized that there are remarkable stories that need to be shared. (You will find a bunch of them in this book). Many leaders were successful because they listened to and learned from their peers. They worked hard to leave the auto mechanic's stereotypical reputation behind them and create professionalism and differentiation in themselves and their business. Leaders are readers, and for many was the differentiator in how successful they became.

The service sector's reputation has grown because owners stopped being a mechanic and became a business owner or CEO. Becoming a CEO is hard work. I've heard about their CEO journey in the hundreds of interviews I've hosted. It didn't take long for me to include business coaches and marketing specialists (like Jennifer Filzen) into the mix to teach new and smarter ways to lead, earn, and market their business.

In my podcasting voyage, I found a willingness from automotive aftermarket professionals to share their continuing journey. As Jennifer discovered and knows, the journey is never complete. We never stop learning. We try, fail, do it again, encourage, lead, and share. This recurring theme is evident in every podcast interview and prevalent in this book. As hundreds of essential

FOREWORD

voices of the automotive aftermarket shared their wisdom, we all became better. Many ships started to rise. And Jennifer is sharing the wisdom she has gathered from her clients and friends to help you.

Jennifer Filzen and I met at AAPEX 2017 at a special dinner hosted by a mutual friend. Immediately I knew I had to interview Jennifer. She had an electrifying way about her. She cared deeply about others and embraced you into her circle. She has been on six podcast episodes to date and always brings her passion for helping people.

The concepts and principles Jennifer shares is a calling for her. She wants to see you succeed at a higher level than you can imagine. You can tell how proud she is to share many of her client's and friend's stories that became a solid foundation for this book's principles.

There comes a time when you know that giving back to those who have made you successful is the next most crucial thing to do in your business and life. Jennifer writes a blueprint of principles and ideas on creating your next big Give to Get Principle.

Today it is OK to get your ideas from others; an important reason we read books. We love suggestions, but we sometimes have trouble implementing them. Jennifer and her clients share their "Give to Get" programs, giving you a quick start. The many ideas shared in this book are there not only to praise but to push you to the implementation stage.

FOREWORD

Don't try to reinvent the wheel. Start. Rip off and duplicate any ideas offered in this book and call it your own. It will never be the same or identical as you make it yours.

Jennifer helps you discover these three important principles you need in your life. Your Why, Your Superpower, and Your Attitude. If you only work on these three, you will improve. As I look back into my over 800 episodes in the podcast library, I can relate to many aftermarket leaders who had these three principles in check and continually work on them.

Jennifer wrote a page-turning book that will, if you let it, help you get to the next level of success, community, and profit. Remember your purpose (why) will reign strongly in your life and business once you embrace its power.

Carm Capriotto
Founder/Host
Aftermarket Radio Network

Remarkable Results Radio Podcast
Town Hall Academy Podcast
Aftermarket Weekly

remarkableresults.biz

Quarter 1: Who Am I & Why Am I Writing This Book?

CHAPTER 1
Introduction

Thank you for picking up this book and reading what I have to say. As a result of you reading this book, you will learn various techniques and stories from other successful business owners to help you turn your clients into raving fans. My goals are to show how to find your WHY, uncover the SUPERPOWERS of you and your team, and the reasons why ATTITUDE makes for loyal clients...even in the darkest of economic times. I will help you define what you are willing to GIVE TO GET, put your systems in place, and share what other shop owners do to develop loyal clients that come back again and again for many years.

I'm looking for auto repair shop owners that want to take their business from surviving to thriving. The ideal reader of this book is someone who wants to grow their business.

Who do you know that could benefit from this book? Could that be you? Could it be a Mastermind group that you coach? Could it be a peer that you are mentoring?

My goal is to show you several ideas and techniques that will help you master your crisis-proof business so you can literally and figuratively weather any storm that affects your business.

INTRODUCTION

Thank you for placing your trust in me and allowing me to be your guide on this journey. I appreciate you. :-)

If you and I have not yet met in person, allow me to introduce myself properly.

I am Jennifer Filzen, the owner of Rock Star Marketing, a content marketing agency that proudly serves the auto repair industry in the United States and Canada. Rock Star Marketing is my business's name because I am a bonafide, certified, GRAMMY-qualified Rock Star.

Yep, that's right! In 2006, when I was going through a divorce, I started fulfilling my lifelong dream of writing songs and created two albums released in 2007 and 2009. Though my music did not win me a GRAMMY, nor did my music make me rich and famous, I managed to accomplish a lot. Not bad for a middle-aged white woman who lived in the suburbs. Not bad for a person who was an early adopter of social media marketing and promoted her two music albums on Facebook, Twitter, and MySpace without the need for a record label. Yes, I spent lots of my own money, and in my marketing classes, I share that no, I never made a lot of money off my music. But, I can proudly say that one of my songs hit it big in the Indian market, thanks to Bohemia's remixed song, the Punjabi gangsta rapper, and I am still collecting royalty checks off of my one-hit-wonder.

INTRODUCTION

When I was promoting my music, it was also the time of the Great Recession that began in 2007. By 2009, the construction company I worked for was having significant issues with the falling housing market, so it was then that I decided to launch Rock Star Marketing. I had these new social media marketing skills. In my enthusiasm, I extolled the virtues of how excellent social media marketing could help small businesses to anyone who would listen! I couldn't help myself! Social media marketing was so exciting. It allowed small companies to make their channels and promote their brands. They no longer had to rely on expensive advertising agencies, television commercials, and costly ads in the Yellow Pages business directory and local newspapers. It was cool being an active participant and evangelist in the early days of the social media industry.

CHAPTER 2
Successful Strategies of the Top Shops

This book has been on my heart for a while. But it took the COVID-19 pandemic for me to finally write it. You see, I had been gathering other people's stories, but I had not yet developed my own story about the Give To Get Principle. I needed the COVID-era to make me walk my walk and talk my talk. I needed the early onset of the COVID crises to help my clients pivot their marketing on a dime and get through Sheltering In Place.

The early days of COVID-19 had so many businesses shut down. The auto repair industry was lucky in that they were considered "essential businesses". But government mandates shut down so many other companies. Restaurants, hair salons, bars, live music venues, theaters, and dance studios were shut down for extended periods. When they could open, it was in bursts and spurts, which put a crimp in everyone's budget. As I write this, we are not yet out of the COVID crisis. We are still in the throes of a global pandemic, and the future of so many remains uncertain.

But it has been during this time of chaos that I knew I had to share the marketing strategies that my clients and I put into place so that our businesses could thrive and not just survive. One of my mentors, Susie Carder, always says that sometimes we are handed gifts wrapped in sandpaper. I feel that the pandemic

THE GIVE TO GET PRINCIPLE

was a gift wrapped in sandpaper. Yes, terrible things happened during the entire year of 2020, but I have a lifelong habit of finding the good in every situation. It was these little rays of hope and silver linings of resilience that made me want to share the golden nuggets we found in this challenging yet pivotal year.

In March 2020, Shelter In Place was put into effect in every state across the nation. Not only was the United States observing the idea of sheltering in place and wearing facemasks, but so were many other countries across the globe. This shutdown affected how people worked, how children attended school, and how people traveled daily. As a result of the shutdown, not many people were driving their cars. Less commuting and fewer people traveling put a lot of my auto repair shop owners into a tailspin of worry.

None of us had ever dealt with a pandemic before, and many business owners didn't know what to do at first. The health authorities advised us to wash our hands more frequently and more thoroughly. We were told to wear facemasks. We figured out how to sanitize the inside of cars, door handles, and steering wheels. We found equipment that would help clean the air. We developed concierge services that would offer contactless pickup, delivery, and payment services so the car owners wouldn't have to leave their homes to get their cars serviced.

We pooled all of our ideas together. When one shop owner came up with a helpful email blast for their clients, I asked if they

THE GIVE TO GET PRINCIPLE

were willing to share their email content with my other shop owner clients. When they said yes, I created an open document that I shared with everyone in my client circle to use the emails, graphics, and social media posts that others had created. Together, we were stronger. Together, we got through the worst months of 2020. Together, we leaned on each other, and we were not alone.

Relationship marketing became the number one factor to success for businesses throughout the COVID-era. If you had developed a strong community of clients who loved you and your work before the pandemic, it was those people who would pull your business through. But let me say this. The companies that struggled before COVID hit had two choices: continue to work or go out of business. Businesses that had solid systems, processes, and a marketing strategy in place survived the pandemic and thrived.

Those businesses that made the extra effort to reach out to their clients were the ones that came out on top. They picked up the phone and called on their database to check in and see how they were doing. As a result, they performed better than other firms who wished and whined their way through the year about how they wanted life to return to normal. After COVID-19 hit, the "normal" way of life was gone forever. The global pandemic changed us all in a short time, and relationships became a currency as powerful as money.

I naturally take the principles of giving to get, of reciprocity, and relationship marketing, and use them in every aspect of my life.

THE GIVE TO GET PRINCIPLE

It is who I am as a person.

In my marketing business, I gave away plenty of time and services to show my clients that I was on this journey with them, and my team was going to be there to support them through thick and thin. Our dance business was closed throughout COVID. However, we continued meeting with our dance community online every Saturday night to check-in, share how we were doing, share some laughs, or have a virtual Happy Hour. Together, we leaned on each other when the fires ravaged California, our job prospects were drying up, or when we mourned the loss of loved ones. Relationships were what brought us joy, got us through the darkest times, and gave us something to look forward to when we could finally be able to dance together again.

The pandemic made us appreciate the little things we so often took for granted pre-pandemic. Before the Coronavirus, we went out to dinner, went shopping and danced all night long. Going to a bar to hear live music and share a cocktail was our norm. All of it was gone. As each month passed, 2020 felt like a year that would never end. January felt like two years ago, and it's only November. I had planned for my 50th birthday bonanza in September 2020 for two years, and all of my plans were thrown out the window. But our relationships and the ability to meet online with friends and family got us through.

2020 is a year none of us will ever forget. But like I said before, it has been a gift wrapped in sandpaper. In this book, I will outline

THE GIVE TO GET PRINCIPLE

what we learned from it all and how all of these things helped us lean into our marketing to make our businesses stronger.

Gloria Gaynor wrote the famous song, "I Will Survive!" That's how a lot of us have been feeling throughout the year. I hope that after reading about the concept of giving to get and building community through reciprocity, you will survive and thrive, too.

CHAPTER 3
Knowing Your Why

I want to share some of the best examples I have heard from my clients about employing the Give To Get Principle. My Rock Star Squad and I have interviewed over 600 small business owners in the auto repair industry alone. They each have uniqueness and a strategic approach to how they give of themselves to acquire raving fans.

My clients are champion-level small business owners. What does it mean to be a champion-level small business owner? They are in the top 10% of their industry as a whole, and they dominate their local market or are poised to do so within a short time frame. I have found that these champion-level small business owners pour their hearts and souls into their businesses. They have shared their stories with my marketing team. Our goal is to get a clear picture of what makes them special and unique, who their target demographic is, and what is their "why". Their "why" is the secret sauce that allows us to create heartfelt content that attracts their ideal customers.

Suppose you're not sure what I mean by learning about their "why". I will paraphrase from Simon Sinek about what he presented in his TED Talk and numerous books. When you know "why" you do something, it takes on a more definite meaning.

THE GIVE TO GET PRINCIPLE

Some say it's a gut feeling, but Simon Sinek explains that it comes from the cerebral cortex, which is an area that doesn't command language but does contain that inner sense of knowing. Sinek goes on to explain that any business can try to sell you on the features and benefits of a product or service. But the reasons why people make those products or run a service business are at the heart of what drives them to get out of bed each day and pursue their passions.

When I teach my marketing classes, I often will ask the business owners about their why. Why do you get out of bed every day, even when you don't want to? Why did you get into this business in the first place? What are you passionate about?

Andy Emery of Antero Automotive & Truck in Greenwood Village, CO is one of my clients. When he was in my marketing class, I asked the question, "What motivates you to get out of bed every day?" His hand shot up. Andy said that his "why" is the opportunity to serve others through his church. He regularly participated in missions that brought water to underdeveloped communities in foreign countries. He also participated in church fundraisers that helped give Christmas presents to the children of people in prison.

Serving others is Andy's "why," and you can see it in everything he does within his business. He does a great job of creating a positive company culture with his team. He goes above and beyond for his clients, who are raving fans. Plus, he has built an

THE GIVE TO GET PRINCIPLE

excellent reputation in his area as a top auto repair shop. Andy is a champion-level small business owner, and his revenue continues to grow because his "why" and desire to serve is so strong.

When the Coronavirus hit in early 2020, Andy was among the group of shop owners that shared his email blasts and social media posts with my other clients. He was among the first of the shop owners to pivot quickly and offer concierge service to his clients so they could get their car repaired with touchless service. Andy and his team sanitized the vehicles, keys, steering wheels, and countertops. He offered pick up and delivery service for any client who wasn't keen on leaving their house. This business owner did everything in his power to make his clients feel safe and comfortable. Andy is a servant leader, and by giving service to his clients, he continues to develop a loyal fan base that provides high recommendations on several review sites.

CHAPTER 4
Building Self Confidence

Today, I am a successful owner of a respected marketing agency that is well recognized within the auto repair industry. But it wasn't always this way.

When I started my marketing agency in 2009, I had to hustle to find clients who wanted to try this new social media marketing thing. Social media platforms like MySpace, Facebook, and Twitter were still in the infancy stage. Our nation was in the middle of the Great Recession, and I left the construction industry to try my hand at running my own marketing business. That first year meant a lot of hard work, tapping into my savings account, and trying to find my ideal clients. That first year of trying something new in a sinking economy was rough, but I knew I had to keep trying because social media marketing held such promise.

It took me about six years before I would start feeling confident that my marketing agency would sustain itself. I remember starting my business in 2009, and by 2014, I felt like I needed to give up. I felt like I needed to get a job somewhere because I could not make enough money each month without tapping into my savings. I took a job at a local hotel, thinking that might be the path towards my destiny. I found out quickly that I was not

THE GIVE TO GET PRINCIPLE

too fond of the job at the hotel.

But the advantage was that I met some wonderful people who came to that hotel for business every week. So, in the six months that I worked at the hotel, these friends of mine continued to forge a relationship with me and repeatedly asked, "Jen, why are you working here?" One of these guys is a friend named Roger Turnau. He said, "You know, Jen, they don't serve fine china at McDonald's. I don't understand why it is that you're working here. You are so much more talented than this. You are limiting yourself. You should stop working here. I'm going to see what I can do about getting you fired."

That was such a wake-up call because I knew that yes, my destiny was to run my marketing agency. But I didn't see at the time how I was going to make it. Finally, in 2015, I quit that job, and I decided to go all-in with my marketing agency. It took me a little while, but business had become stable by the time I reached 2016. In 2017, that was when the floodgates opened for my business. I met a client, Joe Sevart of I-70 Auto Service in Kansas City, MO, who introduced me to approximately 120 other shop owners through his channels and networks. That was when I knew I would have success as a marketing agency that catered to the auto repair industry.

The lessons I learned when those floodgates opened was the power of relationships. When I started my career, I focused on making money. I think most of us do when we start something new. Money is made when you build relationships and stay in

THE GIVE TO GET PRINCIPLE

those relationships over time. Any successful business's goal is to have clients and have a tribe of raving fans who love them and will be loyal for many years. When you can capitalize on your relationships, that is when your business will grow.

What Joe Sevart did for me was open the floodgates for my business. Because we had created a relationship, he knew that I wanted to do everything in my power to help his business succeed. When he saw my authenticity, my enthusiasm for marketing, and my desire to serve, he trusted that I had his best interest at heart. When he saw our results from the marketing work we did, he was so excited about how his revenues were growing. He then told his coach and many of his 20 group members about my business and how I could help them.

I always knew that relationships were essential to business. However, I didn't quite realize how relationships and money connected. I discovered through trial and error that my focus had to change away from money and move closer to developing my relationships. When I focused on the money first, I did not serve the others in my life as best as I could have. But when I focused instead on the relationships being my top priority, that was when the magic happened. I developed a certain level of trust with my clients, who would then become friends. These relationships will help you pull through the good times, the bad times, and everything in between.

More money is made when you build relationships and serve

THE GIVE TO GET PRINCIPLE

others. Servant leaders always outperform because they are about "we" versus "I." Servant leaders are the ones who develop champion-level businesses. I got the term servant leadership from one of my clients, Ernie Skillingstad of Ernie's Inc. in Olympia, WA.

Ernie is one of those Champion business owners that I adore. He and his family operate an RV repair facility in Olympia, Washington. One of the things that he does to solidify his relationship with his client base is to teach new RV owners how to drive them. Especially in the COVID era, many people no longer want to travel on airplanes or cruise ships. Instead, they are renting or purchasing recreational vehicles to continue traveling by driving across the country. Many of his clients are brand new RV owners. They have never driven a motorhome or trailer before. They have never towed any camper behind their vehicle.

When you invest in an RV, it is an expensive investment. You don't want to wreck your brand new acquisition. Some of those magical things that Ernie's Inc. does is offer classes on how to drive an RV, back it up, hitch a trailer to the towing vehicle, and more. Because Ernie and his team offer this service, they have developed a tribe of raving fans. They have RV clients who live outside of Washington State who will drive to Ernie's Incorporated because they know they'll get exceptional customer service.

When I started my marketing agency back in 2009, I was doubtful of my success because I was inexperienced. I knew that through

THE GIVE TO GET PRINCIPLE

social media marketing, I could help other businesses grow. But at that time, I was not sure of what could make a champion-level business. Over time, I learned that telling my clients and their businesses' story would be the first step in attracting their ideal customers and establishing long-lasting relationships with them.

One of the secret weapons we use here at Rock Star Marketing is our SEO interview. The SEO interview is what I utilize to find out who my clients are, what makes them special and unique, and who they wish to serve. A question I always ask my clients is, "What is your why?" When I know why they get out of bed every day to go do their work, I better understand what motivates them.

Over the years, I have discovered that every single client of mine has a different why. Some clients want to be the best in their local market. Some clients want to spend more time with their families. Some clients want to retire and give their time to their church. Some have a lifelong dream of serving those around them. When I know what resonates within their hearts, it is easier for me to tell the story of what makes them special and unique.

When I teach my marketing classes, I will ask the students to write down ten things that make them special and unique. We do this as a group exercise because I want everyone to feel engaged. So, we grab a partner and share the top 10 things that make us special and unique. After everyone writes these ten items down, we share with the class what they wrote. Most of the time, they will pretty much say the same thing. "We are honest. We are

THE GIVE TO GET PRINCIPLE

affordable. We do it right the first time."

The problem is that everyone says those things. These are what all auto repair shops claim to do, and therefore, are not special nor unique. You have to dig a little deeper to find out what is truly special and unique. Every single person on this planet has a uniqueness that they get to share with the world. When you can tap into what makes you unique, that is when you can craft a story about how your uniqueness allows you to serve your clients in the best way possible.

THE GIVE TO GET PRINCIPLE

CHAPTER 5
The Four Currencies

So why am I telling you this? I want you to know it took me a while to figure out that relationships were what I needed to forge before I could thoroughly succeed in my business. I had to learn through trial and error what works and what doesn't. We can read all the business books we want, but until we directly navigate our business relationships, we remain inexperienced.

Recently I heard a business coach talk about the four currencies. The four currencies include money, time, knowledge, and relationships. In my opinion, a lot of business owners start their businesses because they want to focus on the money currency. That makes sense for most business owners. Because we mostly see a focus on money within business cultures, money is the main currency we chase after.

Let's look at the other three currencies. Those are time, knowledge, and relationships. For the time currency, they often say that time is money. If you waste too much time, you're also wasting money.

Knowledge is another currency that we use, especially when we have a skill that is not easy to come by. For example, an inexperienced surgeon may be less expensive but not better than an experienced surgeon. A professional auto mechanic with factory-level equipment and skills can charge more than a less-experienced auto mechanic who works under a shade tree.

The last currency is relationships. I want to focus on relationships. Relationships, especially during the COVID-era, are almost as valuable, if not more valuable, than the money currency.

Going deep in your relationships means more than money at times. Remember, there are four currencies: Money, Time, Knowledge, and Relationships. Relationships bring you the money, time, and knowledge you are seeking. That is why I believe relationships are the most important of all four currencies.

To explain what I mean, let's talk about what happened at the beginning of COVID-19. When the pandemic was first breaking the news, and people started to panic, we had shelter-in-place mandates in most states. People stayed home, not going anywhere and keeping to themselves because no one understood what this virus could do or how you could get it. As a result, a lot of businesses were in a panic, and many industries had to shut down. These industries included restaurants, amusement parks, hair salons, and other non-essential businesses. Like grocery stores, auto repair shops, and hospitals, the essential businesses were the only ones that could stay open in the initial shelter in place ordinances.

When fewer people were walking into your essential business,

THE GIVE TO GET PRINCIPLE

and you were one of those few businesses that were still open, an inevitable panic set in. Many business owners across the nation applied for economic relief and payroll protection plan loans. That infusion of cash was miraculous in some ways and helped a lot of businesses remain stable. However, the panic was still there.

The auto repair shop owners I worked with knew that they would have to make some tough decisions if they were not able to maintain the monthly revenues they grew to depend on. Many of these shop owners called me, asking me how we could market to their client base and get more people to come in for service and repairs. After all, the shop owners have employees to feed, equipment to pay for, and many other overhead costs. Therefore, they needed to have more cars coming in to make sure they could pay their employees and monthly bills.

When I received all of these calls and emails from my client asking for help, I knew I had to do something to support them all in a new way. Andy Emery of Antero Automotive had created an email that he would send out to his client base and asked me to proofread it for him. It was a great email, and I asked Andy if I could share it with everybody to use that as a template. He said yes.

The next day, I received another email created by Bob Cornwall of Placentia Super Service in Placentia, CA. Bob's email had a few more points that we're different from Andy's email. Both emails were fantastic. I asked Bob if it was okay with him if I

THE GIVE TO GET PRINCIPLE

shared his email template with my client base, and he said yes.

For the next few months, we would do this for our clients. We would pool our ideas and knowledge and templates together and share them with everybody that worked with me. I gave away a lot of time and free resources to my clients because, as I told them then and continue to say now, we are stronger when we work together, and we will get through this together, and we did.

I've wanted to write this book for a while. Over the past decade, I have interviewed many clients who are super successful. But there was something that kept delaying me from writing this book. Now that we are in the throes of a lingering global pandemic, I know what made me pause. I needed to experience the Give To Get Principle myself first, before I could aptly tell other people's stories. I needed to live through the challenges myself. Because I also had to pivot, depend upon my relationships, and remain flexible through uncertain times, the experience allowed me to deliver my message more confidently and clearly to my readers.

I want you to see how special you are. I want you to see how your business is unique. I want you to know that you can develop raving fans through the love, service, and care you give as a business owner. Every single time I interview a new client, I hear how they have created a successful business. These interviews have taught me how to run my business successfully. To honor them, I knew that I had to share the success of reciprocity and the Give To Get Principle. Relationships are super critical to the

THE GIVE TO GET PRINCIPLE

success of a business. My goal is to show reciprocity in action and how it benefits the bottom line of business. I believe that when you put relationships first, the money will follow.

Quarter 2: What Is The Problem and What Are The Solutions?

Many business owners understand the benefits of the Give To Get Principle, but they don't know where to start. This section is designed to identify the opportunities all businesses face when establishing deeper connections to their client base.

CHAPTER 6
The Difference Between You And The Top 10%

If there is a significant problem I see in small businesses, it is the lack of training in relationship building. Personal development helps people be mindful of their feelings around self-worth, their income-earning potential, daring to live the life of their dreams, and creating their best life. But how many entrepreneurs go into business with personal development training as a priority? The answer is smaller than you think.

Most entrepreneurs want to start a business because they have big goals and lots of passion. That is fantastic! Those are two key ingredients to developing a successful business. But not a lot of companies make it. Many don't last beyond five years.

If you want to rise through your local market and your industry ranks, you need to work on personal development to break through the challenges you put in your way. To get to the top, you need to establish sustainable systems and processes, remove the chaos, know your worth, invest in training, and have the end goal in mind. My hope for you is to help you make it into the top 10% of your industry at the very minimum. But if I'm going to help you get there, you need to get beyond just surviving. You need to get to a place of thriving!

THE GIVE TO GET PRINCIPLE

Identifying the problems and solutions in relationship marketing is something all business owners should be mindful of daily. Many businesses do not make it to the top ten percent in their industry. Why? Perhaps they are not paying attention to the relationship marketing that is going on internally and externally. Chances are fairly good that if their business is not succeeding, they are not investing in their relationships and applying the Give To Get Principle.

The bottom 90% is a significant number. I'm sure you're saying, "Jen, I have so many more important things to worry about. Why should I give a crap about my relationships with my employees? I pay them to work, and all I want them to do is show up on time and do their jobs."

Listen, I get it. As the business owner, you may be frustrated when your team doesn't perform to the level they should. But remember this. People who love what they do, enjoy their company culture, and like their coworkers tend to do better jobs. Happy employees are far more productive and reliable than those working in a toxic, overly competitive, or neglectful workplace.

Think about the best boss you've ever had. What did that boss do to make you feel good about your work? How did this person convey that he or she cared about you and your well-being? When you worked for this great boss, were you excited to go to work, or did you dread it?

THE GIVE TO GET PRINCIPLE

The chances are high that you started your business because you didn't want to be treated poorly anymore or not get paid well enough. Speaking for myself, I wanted to make sure I owned my business so I could never get laid off again. Now that I have owned my business for over a decade, I realize that though I may not get fired by my boss, which is myself, I can get rejected by my clients, my employees, my affiliate partners, my vendors, and more. I have to work even harder as a business owner than I did as an employee.

Over time, I started to see and appreciate what my old bosses did. Right or wrong, there were reasons they said or did things that upset me. They called me out on things that make me cringe, now that I am that business owner. Ah, to be young and naive again!

As you spend more time running your business, you may begin to see through the lens of what your previous managers looked through. To share an example, I was recently in a challenging situation with an employee. I do everything I can to foster a warm, friendly, supportive, and happy company culture. We support each other and work as a unit to get our projects completed on or ahead of schedule.

This one employee was continually delivering content at the very last minute. Each time I talked with her about it, her excuses were good enough that I let things slide. This continued for several months until she missed three deadlines in one week. When I met with her, I told her that I liked her, I was pleased with her

THE GIVE TO GET PRINCIPLE

work quality, but when she missed our deadlines, she broke our company's number one rule. I had to let her go. Why? Because if I didn't, it would create a death-by-a-thousand-cuts scenario with my team, and it would make a toxic team environment. I did it to protect the greater good of our internal relationships.

Do you recall any employee situations where one employee created tension and strife among your team? If you've been around long enough, I'm sure you've seen it or experienced it before.

Look, relationship marketing and the Give To Get Principle apply to your internal team, customers, and even your vendors.

So let me ask you this: Are you forging good relationships with all three groups? If not, why aren't you?

Businesses that neglect the Give To Get Principle need help if they want to survive, let alone thrive, and grow into something sustainable. When you make an effort to develop those relationships, your business will succeed for sure. After all, teamwork makes the dream work.

If you could create a dream team that works for you, you will create a workspace that has positive energy. When your vendors and clients experience your team's positive energy, they are more likely to place their trust in them. Like attracts like, and the Law of Attraction proves that when the employees are happy in their jobs, they are more likely to provide exceptional customer service

THE GIVE TO GET PRINCIPLE

and quality workmanship. If they're unhappy, they may act out in small and large ways that sabotage the success of your business.

The next time one of your employees is habitually late for work, or they seem less than excited to be at their desk, try to find out the root cause so you can address it. If they know you care and you are there to lift them up, they will seek your praise and do everything they can to make you happy. When you focus on creating a great company culture, you are on your way to rising through your industry ranks.

THE GIVE TO GET PRINCIPLE

CHAPTER 7
Whys + Superpowers + Attitude = Raving Fans

My goal is to have you examine your business from a fresh perspective. To begin, let's look at three simple questions that are designed to make you think more deeply:

What is your "why"?
What is your "superpower"?
What is your "attitude"?

These three little questions are the key to your success in attracting your ideal customers and converting them into raving fans. If you want your business to grow, you need to keep these three questions in mind.

What is your "why"?

When you know what drives you, a lot of your business goals become more apparent. When you can pinpoint the things that motivate you to succeed, you'll be more confident in moving toward those goals so you can be sure of your results. Your mindset will shift from "I wish I could be better" to "I am making headway and seeing my progress over time."

THE GIVE TO GET PRINCIPLE

I teach marketing classes, and I always talk about finding your "Why" through the lens of Simon Sinek. If you have never heard of this fantastic author, speaker, and thought leader, I encourage you to do a quick search on YouTube and watch his TED Talks.

Next, I want you to do a self-assessment. What is your why? Some of us have a personal why and a professional why. Others have one big why that motivates them. The good news is that there are no wrong answers about your why. It's YOUR why, after all, and it may evolve as you grow older.

But when we operate from our personal and professional why, there is a certainty we feel deep in our gut. When you are in this state of knowing, how do you feel when operating from this place of higher purpose? Do you feel calm? Excitement? Motivation? Perhaps a twinge of fear? All of the above?

Don't worry. You are not alone. But so few people take the time to identify their why. If you are unclear what your why is, let me give you an example. Let's look at John Eppstein, an incredibly successful independent auto repair shop owner in San Diego.

John Eppstein of John's Automotive Care in San Diego
  Personal Why: Pursuit of excellence and maintain top-dog status

  Professional Why: Always thinking outside of the box to develop his customer pipeline

  Give To Get: Kids' treasure chest in his office, holds a very

THE GIVE TO GET PRINCIPLE

successful toy drive for the Boys and Girls Clubs of East County, offers mentoring and scholarship funds for teens pursuing automotive technician careers

John is accustomed to being a dominant leader in his local market. San Diego is a highly competitive market, so he has to stay in his A Game. That is why John's professional why is thinking outside of the box to develop his customer pipeline. This why is the driving force behind his success.

The method he employs in his Give To Get strategy is to participate in things that help kids. He offers toys and games from the treasure chest he keeps in his office, and those kids get to take them home. He also has a toy drive that benefits the Boys and Girls Clubs of East County. But the real gem of his giving concept is the mentoring and scholarship funds for teenagers who want to pursue a career in the automotive industry. He is single-handedly nurturing the next generation of car owners and automotive technicians.

Guess who asks their parents to take the car in for an oil change every six months so they can get a new toy? The kids. Guess who wants to join the Boys and Girls Clubs of East County so they can learn fun things about cars? The kids. Guess who will develop a love for all things automotive when they get the opportunity to work with their hands, solve technical challenges, and feel a sense of accomplishment when they brought a dead car back to life? The kids. That's a great why.

THE GIVE TO GET PRINCIPLE

Speaking of kids, here is another example of a business owner who clearly understands his "why":

Joe Sevart of I-70 Auto Service in Kansas City, MO

<u>Personal Why:</u> His family and grandkids are Joes's why. He strives to be the best possible business owner so he can provide for his family and spoil his grandkids.

<u>Professional Why:</u> Provide a stress-free customer service experience.

<u>Give To Get:</u> Courtesy pick up and delivery service, and a free candy bar of your choice when you come into the shop after your vehicle is repaired.

So, what is your why? I encourage you to write it down on a small piece of paper and carry it around in your wallet so you can see it frequently. This visual reminder of your why will motivate you daily to make your goals happen.

What is your "superpower"?

Next, let's talk about your superpower. When a company culture encourages each team member to play to their strengths, the chances are high that you will see a happier, top-performing team. People like to be encouraged to do what they love, and that makes them want to show up on time, do an excellent job for those they serve, and get excited about the projects they're working on.

THE GIVE TO GET PRINCIPLE

Suppose you want to manifest a work environment that has positive energy, improved teamwork, and a terrific customer service experience. In that case, I encourage you to reflect on these questions about your superpowers and those of your staff:

- Do you automatically know what your talents and strengths are?

- Do you have one superpower that no one else can beat?

- Or, do you have a combination of strengths that make you a superhero in one area?

- Following that, what are the superpowers of your team members?

- Do you know their strengths?

- What talents do they bring to the party?

- Do they excel at solving the most challenging problems?

- Are they exceptional in turning a frown upside down?

- Are they great listeners?

- Are they top performers?

THE GIVE TO GET PRINCIPLE

Please give it some thought and see what comes to mind. But with great superpowers, there is usually some kryptonite that balances it out.

- What is your weakness?

- What are the weaknesses of your team?

- Do those weaknesses stop your superpowers from showing up altogether, or are the drawbacks reasonably minor?

- When you take a close look at your customer reviews, how many five-stars do you get compared to 1-star reviews? What's the average?

- Do you need to figure out how to tip the balance within your team, so their strengths outweigh the weaknesses?

It would be wise for you to assess what is going on with the superpowers and kryptonite of you and your team.

I have two examples of auto repair shop owners that have identified their superpowers: Steve Mancinelli and Sherri Stock.

Steve Mancinelli of Mancinelli's Auto Repair Center
 Personal Superpower: Steve is a 3rd generation shop owner and has a family reputation to protect. He has tenacity and determination as his personal superpower. He stood up against

THE GIVE TO GET PRINCIPLE

the corporations in downtown Denver, who were buying up the land around him and developing the area.

Professional Superpower: Steve works hard to serve his clients and neighbors. Because his family has been serving Denver for 3 generations, he is all about nurturing and supporting his local community. Additionally, his company offers a 5-year/50,000-mile warranty, which is a gold-standard warranty for our industry.

Give To Get: Mancinelli's Auto Repair Center in downtown Denver hosts annual BBQs, pet adoption fundraisers, and bags of microwave popcorn that say "Thanks for Popping By".

Sherri Stock of InMOTION Auto Care in Lincoln, NE

Personal Superpower: Sherri has had a longtime career in the auto repair industry, getting her start at the Chrysler dealership. Being a woman in a male-dominated field, she has shown dogged determination to excel as a business owner.

Professional Superpower: Sherri and her team strive to deliver the best auto repair customer-service experience possible. inMOTION Auto Care goes above and beyond when it comes to building a relationship with every customer who drives into their Lincoln facility. They also offer a 5-year/50,000-mile warranty.

Give To Get: Sherri Stock has a garden in the back of her

THE GIVE TO GET PRINCIPLE

shop, as well as a professional kitchen and smoker inside her shop. She feeds her staff and she also shares her harvest with her clients.

As you can see, Steve and Sherri have different superpowers. But they each play to their strengths and use those strengths to provide an exceptional customer service experience. Their clients adore them, and many are raving fans who tell everyone in their social circle about their favorite mechanic.

Can you see how knowing your personal and professional superpowers can help your business grow? Next, let's look at the third question:

What is your "attitude"?

Once you know the answers about everyone's superpowers and kryptonite, then you can assess the third topic: Attitude. I have a few questions for you, and I'd like you to reflect on them for a moment:

- Is your attitude generally positive or negative?

- How about the individual attitudes within your team?

- Is your work environment a happy company culture?

- Are some team members friendly and professional while other team members are lacking those traits?

THE GIVE TO GET PRINCIPLE

- Do you have a toxic work culture?

- If the attitude in your business is less-than-desirable, what are you doing to change it?

Believe it or not, your team's attitude creates noticeable energy that your customers can feel. Customers can immediately feel the difference when they walk into any business. They know when the employees are happy to be there or wishing they were somewhere else. They can see it in the smiles or furrowed brows. They can hear the joyful greetings or short and terse phone calls. They can feel the energy of a clean, cared-for space or a dirty and cluttered workspace. Your customers may not fully articulate the energy they feel from your business, but they can usually boil it down into a few words when writing customer reviews.

To figure out what the public perceives your attitude, take a look at your customer reviews. What are the three things your customers say about you over and over again? Do they say you're friendly? Professional? Cheap? Expensive? Impressive? Disappointing? Reliable? Sketchy? When you take a good look at your reviews, you'll get a good idea about which attitude you and your team are projecting with each customer interaction.

THE GIVE TO GET PRINCIPLE

Here are two examples of small businesses that exhibit a great attitude:

Carl & Maureen Hutchinson of Complete Automotive in Springfield, MO

<u>Personal Attitude:</u> Carl and Maureen are a happily married couple that own a shop in Springfield, Missouri. They deeply believe in God and they deeply care for their community. They have a family of adopted and natural-birth children. They are big believers in giving back to their community. For example, Carl donates blood and blood platelets to the blood bank once a month.

<u>Professional Attitude:</u> Both Carl and Maureen wear their hearts and their love for people on their sleeves. For example, Maureen is very creative and always celebrating the birthdays and work anniversaries of their team members. Their motto is "We Love What We Do" and Carl's email signature reveals his love for God.

<u>Give To Get:</u> Complete Automotive regularly participates in drawings and contests that giveaway gift baskets and jars of candy to clients. They are active in local charities, ministries, and Brakes for Breasts.

Patrick & Linda Dolder of PALS Ocala Auto Repair in Ocala, Florida

<u>Personal Attitude:</u> Patrick and Linda Dolder own PALS

THE GIVE TO GET PRINCIPLE

(Patrick And Linda'S). They have a General Manager named Chuck Perry. Together, they create an amazing "can-do" team attitude. For example, Linda & Patrick are very devout Christians who actively sponsor and support numerous non-profits in their community. Chuck has an attitude of "there is nothing we can't fix". But their personal attitudes come from overcoming personal tragedies which include rectal cancer, the premature death of a child, and going to federal prison.

Professional Attitude: Together, their attitude makes them a champion-level team and everyone on the whole team happily works together and meets or exceeds their numbers every quarter. For example, they get a lot of tourists and snowbirds coming through their area, so they work on everything from horse trailers and RVs to Slingshots and classic car restoration. They're currently working on a 1966 Corvette restoration that is an $80K project.

Give To Get: They are big believers in "Southern Hospitality" and cook up burgers and hot dogs on the grill every Saturday; offering them for free to their clients. A percentage of their net sales goes to sponsor the Boys & Girls Club, The Humane Society, American Cancer Society, St. Jude's Children's Hospital, and more.

If you want your business to thrive, grow, and rise to the top of your market, it would be wise to make sure your company operates with a clear "why," your team is playing to their

THE GIVE TO GET PRINCIPLE

strengths. They can tap into their superpowers, and you foster a positive, can-do attitude. When you combine all three elements, you get a caring culture.

Whether or not you have a caring culture impacts turnover. It impacts enjoyment levels in the workplace, quality workmanship, and outcomes that appear later in your team members' careers. All of that really can be tied back to the type of culture and the type of work environment that you have. When you have a positive, inspired, and motivated team, you're going to work together better naturally. You're going to make friends with each other, and you're going to have high participation in voluntary things or ideas that are being shared.

A caring culture will increase the quality of what you're providing as a group. Your team, your vendors, your clients, and your community at large will respond to the caring culture you cultivate. All of that will increase the bottom line and determine whether or not you can continue in your business. It's a big circle. Your company culture impacts your service quality, affects the revenue growth, and impacts who you can hire. A caring culture can tap into your "why," and it plays up the superpowers and positive attitudes that keep going around and around. Therefore, you'll have a caring culture benefiting everyone it touches.

To add, one of the business owners in my coaching tribe, Lee Richter, said the following about attitude and how important it is to your business. She said that you are renting the behavior of

THE GIVE TO GET PRINCIPLE

your employees. If you are paying expensive rent, per se, is the attitude, skills, and drive of your employee in alignment with that high price?

Lee further stated that your employees have three jobs: 1) To reduce your stress, 2) Make your business money, and 3) Save your business some money. When an employee has a poor attitude and affects how he or she performs these three jobs for your business, you should release them so they can find an opportunity that better fits their goals. Otherwise, the behavior you are renting from them is not performing well and is doing a disservice to your business.

CHAPTER 8
Penguins & Auto Repair Shops

I want to help you grow your business by sharing fantastic examples of what other business owners have done. Because we have written the Search Engine Optimized website content for over 700 companies in 10 years, we have heard many stories related to the Give To Get Principle. If you can learn what other successful businesses do to wow their customers and turn them into raving fans, that is of great value.

When we sit down with a client for two hours to discuss what makes them unique, their "why," and who their target demographic is, they share many golden nuggets with us. In those two hours, they might share a story about how they made someone's life better, how their team solved a challenging problem, or how they make their clients feel super special. Their unique story helps them stand apart from their competitors.

I will often ask the following question when I teach my marketing classes: "Do you know how to tell the difference between a boy and a girl penguin?" When I ask this, not many people do. I don't know how to tell the difference either, and I volunteered at the penguin exhibit for a few years at the Monterey Bay Aquarium! If it weren't for the armbands that told me their names and gender, I still wouldn't be able to differentiate between the males and females.

THE GIVE TO GET PRINCIPLE

But you know what? Penguins see the difference between who is a boy and who is a girl. Penguins understand who is who within their flock. The males have an adorable courtship ritual where they bring pebbles to the female they desire, delivering the resources she needs to prove to her that he's an agile pebble collector and nest builder. He grabs a pebble with his beak, and he lays that pebble at her feet, as a wonderfully romantic gesture. The male who brings the most pebbles tends to win the pragmatic heart of his mate.

Well, when you are courting your ideal customers, you need to stand out from the competition. In the case of auto repair shops, many of them look the same to car owners. They have similar colors, which are blue, red, and black. Plus, they tend to market themselves as honest, reliable, and "we do it right the first time."

Yeah? So what? Every shop says the same thing. They all look alike. How will you stand out from the crowd and woo your ideal client? Instead of laying a pebble at their feet, what will you give?

To illustrate my point about standing out from the crowd, here are a few examples of what my clients do to nurture their client relationships:

- Ole's Car Shop in Palo Alto, CA -- The owner retired for several years and passed away in 2020 after losing his diabetes and COPD battle. But when I first met Ole Christiansen around 2005, he did the most incredible thing for Honda

THE GIVE TO GET PRINCIPLE

owners whose cars had over 300,000 miles. Ole would give a birthday cake, complete with a candle, so the owner could blow it out and make a wish. The idea was to celebrate that the owner and the repair team did such an excellent job with preventive maintenance that these cars would last for many miles on the same engine. This gesture thrilled the Honda owners! They felt praised for doing a great job maintaining their vehicles. In return, Ole's Automotive got many customer referrals and a client base of loyal fans.

- Premier Auto Service Center of Southwest Florida in Cape Coral, FL -- Emile and Jocelyne Dauphinais love to support their community. They do so in several ways. A portion of their sales proceeds is dedicated to scrips money going to various public schools. If you wanted a specific school to receive the scrips funds, you would name the recipient school, and Jocelyne would keep a running tab of which schools acquired the designated amounts. Every quarter, a report is done and a check is made for each designated school. They also host fundraisers for people living with cancer. Jocelyne is a cancer survivor, so she wants to support others who are battling for their lives. Plus, Emile and Jocelyne regularly host Cruise-Ins, where the car enthusiasts drive over to hang out and eat hot dogs & burgers cooked by the staff. They are all about community, and it's no wonder why their shop has a dedicated following.

THE GIVE TO GET PRINCIPLE

- D&H Enterprises and Cars 2nd Chance in Concord, CA -- D&H Enterprises is owned by a married couple, Mary and Dave Kemnitz, who are also proud members of Rotary International. In the early years of owning their auto repair shop, they consistently had a few customers who had vehicles that were not worth investing in and wanted to donate them. The customers requested Dave and Mary's help with locating a nonprofit charity to take the cars. After investigating which charity had the best reputation, they discovered that all the charities took at least 70% of the proceeds for administrative fees. Realizing that their own Rotary Club had a nonprofit arm, they decided to create their car donation center. With the help of their own Rotary Club members volunteered the administrative work so that 99% of the profits could go right back into helping others. Dave, Mary, and the Rotary Club agreed with Copart Auto Auctions to take the donated vehicles to auction. Thus began Cars2ndChance, which has brought $1.2 million to the Rotary since its origin in 2010. C2C has branched out in many ways, marketing for donations for many causes; 60 Cars were reconditioned at their business and sent to Paradise after the fires decimated the entire City. Today, over $50K has been donated to the Foodbank of Contra Costa and Solano Counties since the onset of the Covid Pandemic. Many cars have been reconditioned through the years and given to individuals in need within the community.

THE GIVE TO GET PRINCIPLE

- C&G Auto Center in Orlando, FL -- This repair shop is owned by The Ramirez Family that migrated from the Dominican Republic. The majority of clients aren't like clients to them; they're like family. Their mother is a big reason they exhibit the Give To Get Principle. The waiting room is kid-friendly, with cartoons, lollipops, and candy. They have a big family of their own, so they know that having something for the kids is helpful to the parents. Mom was a teacher before joining the shop, and when she has the opportunity, she'll start teaching the kids about car care and share ideas with the parents where the kids can go for better education. But, Mom talks more than just about cars. The immediate community is mostly Latino and Black. They offer their community more than only car repairs. If you need a lawyer, they can help. Immigration help? Give them a call. Besides their car, they can help with careers, too. It's like family. It pays dividends because their shop is considered a revered resource among their Orlando neighbors.

- Suburb Service in Lake Forest Park, WA -- Candy Johns was the heart and soul of this Subaru specialty shop in the North Seattle area. She died suddenly of a heart attack in 2020, but her co-owner husband, Howard Musolf, and their General Manager, Debra Christner, continue to run the business that Candy built with such love and care. Candy actively participated in all kinds of charity events, from coordinating Seattle Seahawks Booster Club projects and raising money for school children to the occasional free repair service and

THE GIVE TO GET PRINCIPLE

donation of a wheelchair-access van to disabled clients. Now that Candy is gone, their motto is, "What Could Candy Do?" If a client needs a ride to the eye doctor, they'll do it. If the local dog rescue group requires supplies, they'll donate it. Being an active member of their community and supporting those who are less fortunate is what drives them to be the oldest, largest, and best Subaru shop in the entire Pacific Northwest.

- Bimmer Rescue in Richmond, VA -- Patrick McHugh is a fantastic shop owner that also does a lot for his community. He hosts art gallery openings in his lobby to celebrate and promote a local artist every quarter. He and his crew will dress up the entire waiting area, transforming it into an art gallery. They even set up cocktail tables with tablecloths, hire food trucks to feed the crowds for free and invite everyone in the community to their party. It creates a beautiful, festive atmosphere and their clients love connecting with everyone in a social setting. In the back, the technicians are giving tours of the shop to everyone, including other mechanics who work at different places. When Bimmer Rescue is hiring, they are sure to show those technicians all the great equipment and tools they use, the training programs they utilize, and so on. As a result, they accomplish two things with each art gallery opening: They create a deeper connection with their community and use it as a recruiting tool.

What Are You Willing To Give To Get?

THE GIVE TO GET PRINCIPLE

Every shop that operates at a champion level continues to grow its business by doing some giveaway. They do this to stand apart from the other shops. Some give cookies, and some offer free loaner cars. At the same time, others host customer appreciation barbecue parties or donate proceeds from each sale to local nonprofits.

So, let me ask you this: What are you willing to give? What can you offer that no one else does?

- Is it a nice cup of cappuccino that prints out a customized message for each customer?
- Is it a treasure chest full of toys that allow each child to take one of those toys home?
- How about a charity fundraiser that will enable clients to adopt a dog from a local animal shelter?
- Is it a refrigerator full of soda pop from various regions and countries that is offered to clients for free?
- Is it a pickup and delivery service, so your clients don't have to leave their home or office?
- How about attending RV Rallies across the nation and offering free inspections so you can alert the owners if there is a loose sway bar or if other potential mechanical hazards?
- Is it offering snow cones or ice cream on a hot summer day?
- What about leaving a small package of freshly baked cookies on the dashboard when you deliver the repaired vehicle to your client?

THE GIVE TO GET PRINCIPLE

What are you willing to give to get? What is a low-cost item or service that you can give away to make your clients' lives easier and happier?

My mentor, Joe Fletcher, taught us this when we started the West Coast Swing Dance Company. I can still hear him say this phrase to me in his matter-of-fact, slightly gravelly voice. "You have to give to get. When you give them something, they will feel like they owe you a favor, and they'll be obliged to give you something back." Call it reciprocity or relationship marketing. I call it the Give To Get Principle. It is an exchange of time or goods that benefits everyone involved. It's a simple concept. But if you want to be successful, you have to do it in such a way that it is a little more creative. A little more memorable. A bit more fun. Once you have that, you are on your way to creating a tribe of raving fans who tell everyone how awesome you and your business are to their friends and family. And so it goes, just like a ripple effect of positive energy flowing out in all directions to everyone it touches. And those waves of joy rippling out eventually flow back in towards you like waves of abundance. You win, and everybody wins when you care enough to invest in your relationships.

Remember this: Marketing is an attitude, not a department.

- Marketing is seen when a dentist's office welcomes their patients with a friendly and relaxing dental experience.
- Marketing becomes a tangible thing when you go to the ice cream parlor, and they give away small taste samples so you can try several flavors before you buy two scoops.

THE GIVE TO GET PRINCIPLE

- Marketing is the trust you build with a family who needs to place their children in your childcare center while they are working.

- Marketing is the promise of a leak-free commercial roof that also reflects light and lowers your energy bill.

- Marketing is seen on all the different labels on wine bottles at the liquor shop, allowing you to choose between the pretty labels, the funny labels, and the classy brands that suit your mood at the moment.

- Marketing is the hope that when you work with a particular Information Technology company, your cybersecurity is rock solid, and you won't have to worry about hackers.

- Marketing is seen on roadside billboards inviting you to call a tough law firm if you get into a motorcycle accident.

- Marketing promises to hit the open road and live a life of affordable adventures in a recreational vehicle.

- Marketing is when a business coach tells you all the systems and processes you need to put into place if you want your Facebook advertising campaign to have a positive Return On Investment.

- Marketing is how you answer the phone and engage in conversation with your prospective clients.

- Marketing is how you dress, what you drive, and how you represent the company you work for, and your circle of friends.

- Marketing is getting that extra-generous scoop of popcorn at the movie theater from the concession stand.

Yes, indeed. Marketing is an attitude. It's the promise of the customer service experience. Marketing is all about creating relationships and attracting your ideal clients.

THE GIVE TO GET PRINCIPLE

What are you willing to do within your company to provide an exceptional customer service experience? Your answer is in direct correlation with your level of success. Those businesses that are willing to go the extra mile will win over those who don't. It's that simple.

THE GIVE TO GET PRINCIPLE

CHAPTER 9
Giving & Relationship Marketing

When I first thought of writing this book, I only planned to share the stories of my many auto repair clients. But COVID-19 created an opportunity beyond what I had planned. It allowed me to see past the freebies and goodies my clients handed to their customers.

With fresh eyes, I could see the depth of relationship marketing and how those long-term ties would come to fruition through challenging times. COVID-19, and the economic crisis that ensued, reinforced this idea of the Give To Get Principle because business owners could count on their existing clients for mutual support.

One small but straightforward example was the idea of calling up clients and checking in on their well-being. The goal was not to sell them anything. The sole purpose was to check-in, see if they were okay, and ask if there was anything we could do for them.

Are they older and at risk of contracting the virus, but they were quarantined and unable to get groceries? If yes, did they need us to run to the store on their behalf?

Do they need rolls of toilet paper? Do they need face masks? Do they need a travel kit that includes hand sanitizer, two face masks, and a small package of tissues?

THE GIVE TO GET PRINCIPLE

When we reach out to our Tribe and offer service from the heart, we actively give our time, love, and attention. When someone cares about you, and you know they are doing it because they want to -- not because they have to -- how does that make you feel? I know it makes me feel great when the businesses I favor take great care of me.

I see this type of Give To Get behavior in restaurants all the time. My husband and I love going out to eat because neither one of us prefer to cook. As a result, we get to know the restaurant owners and their staff. We are regulars, and we like to show our support by tipping them well. What do they do for us when we show appreciation for their efforts? Not that it's required, but when they see us coming, they roll out the red carpet. They give us a table without the need for a reservation. They give us an appetizer, free of charge. They remember our drink orders and ask if we would like our regular meals. When we celebrate a birthday, anniversary, or another special occasion, they give us a free dessert.

You've experienced similar treatment in restaurants, I'm sure. Most restaurants I know of typically do something nice for patrons who are celebrating birthdays. It happens all the time.

What can you do in your business that is the equivalent of what restaurants do to keep their customers happy? When you can dial that into your regular Standard Operating Procedures, you are

THE GIVE TO GET PRINCIPLE

well on your way to making each client a fan who tells everyone they know about their positive experience with your company.

Quarter 3: Relationship Marketing Benefits

THE GIVE TO GET PRINCIPLE

CHAPTER 10
We All Scream For Ice Cream

This book has been something I've wanted to write for several years. I wish I had written it sooner. But I kept putting it off because it didn't feel right. Little did I know back then that I would need to live through the COVID-19 pandemic to really "get it." I knew the Give To Get Principle all this time, but I needed to live it myself.

Still, I wish I had written this book sooner because I know there are small business owners out there who could have used the wisdom in this book yesterday!

You may feel that owning a business during a chaotic economy is a struggle. Or you may not have a lot of hope right now, and you feel stuck. But if you adopt the Give To Get Principle, you will see your generosity work in your favor. Expect to see increased revenue for your business.

To illustrate my point, let's talk about ice cream shops. Have you ever gone into an ice cream shop and drooled over the many flavors you see in the freezer case? The bright colors, the cute signs, and the creative names are all designed to make you crave ice cream.

THE GIVE TO GET PRINCIPLE

When you are looking at the menu or freezer case, you aren't sure if you want the coffee ice cream, the pumpkin spice ice cream, or the chocolate swirl ice cream with brownie chunks in it. You ask the attendant if you can have a sample of each flavor to make your decision. The attendant scoops a little taste of each flavor and hands it over to you to try. You try all three, and you decide that since you like two out of the three, you go with double scoops on a waffle cone.

Maybe next time you're visiting, you'll go with the third flavor you didn't choose this time around. But as for this purchase, you thought you were going to go with one scoop, but you decided on two, and you opted for the more expensive waffle cone since the sugar cone would have a more challenging time supporting the two scoops.

Does this sound familiar? Have you ever experienced this type of situation sampling ice cream? I know I sure have, many times over!

The ice cream shop used the Give To Get Principle. They willingly gave you three flavor samples, knowing that they may lose out entirely. You may walk away, not wanting anything. But the chances are high that if you ask for a sample, they'll at least sell you one, and maybe two scoops of ice cream. That's pretty normal for an ice cream shop.

Now, let's pretend we are going to an ice cream shop where samples are not given. Let's pretend that the ice cream shop

THE GIVE TO GET PRINCIPLE

owner takes a look at all of the cartons of ice cream they can sell and all of the money they saved by not giving away anything. This ice cream shop owner feels confident that the ice cream is so superior that people don't need samples and they should trust the fact that it's good and that you should trust them when they say so.

So, you walk into that ice cream shop and ask to sample three flavors. The attendant says sorry, but they don't give out free samples. You aren't sure about the unusual flavors, and you're less likely to risk spending money on a flavor you may not like. So, you opt to buy one scoop of chocolate swirl ice cream with brownie chunks on a sugar cone, and that's it. Why? Because it's safe and somewhat predictable.

How do you feel when you walk away from the second ice cream shop?

- Do you feel like they are enthusiastic about sharing their ice cream? No?
- Do you feel like they were going the extra mile to make you a huge fan of their lesser-known flavors? No?
- Do you feel like you saved some money because you didn't go for that extra scoop? Yes?

I don't know about you, but I want to be a repeat customer of the first ice cream shop and not the second. What about you? Which ice cream shop would you prefer? Which would you tell your friends about?

THE GIVE TO GET PRINCIPLE

We see this type of Give To Get reciprocity in ice cream shops, wineries, and Costco. Heck, I know several people who have gone to Costco during their lunch break so they can get a small meal from all the free samples! But even when they give free samples at Costco, it's hard to leave there without dropping some serious bucks!

With that said, what can you give away to the customers that won't cost you a lot but will build a loyal following? Is it your time? What about bumper stickers or a food item? How about a rewards program for frequent buyers? Or maybe a simple thank you note?

I challenge you to write down three things right now that you can give away that will likely earn you happier clients and more money over the long term. *Go ahead. I'll wait. :-)*

THE GIVE TO GET PRINCIPLE

CHAPTER 11
The COVID Effect

Hey VaynerNation!

A lot of you are shitting on 2020, but in reality it's the year that made you reflect, increased your self awareness, maybe it exposed you to new opportunities. It's the year that woke you up...and that will lead to your ultimate happiness. You just don't know it yet.

♥ ♥ ♥ ♥ ♥

A social media post from Gary Vaynerchuk in 2020.

As I take a cold, hard look at what has transpired in 2020, I have mixed emotions. Part of me wants to laugh at how much I thought

THE GIVE TO GET PRINCIPLE

I had control over things that are not in my possession and never have been. The other part of me wants to cry because I mourn the loss of so many lives due to the pandemic, the loss of many jobs, hardships caused by job loss, and heartbreak for the losses of innocent people. I laugh at the vision board I created for myself in January 2020, filled with hopes and dreams for exotic voyages on cruise ships, increased business revenue, and attending more dance conventions. Oh, how things have changed.

Local businesses and industries worldwide were affected one way or another in 2020 due to the COVID pandemic. The shelter-in-place ordinances, social distancing, many natural disasters across the globe, social unrest, and the tanking economy have affected us all. COVID hurt a lot of businesses, including our dance business. However, every bad thing that happens to us offers an opportunity to pivot and learn how to find solutions. For example, I learned how to shift within my marketing business and help more small businesses thrive in harsh economic times. I leaned into my marketing efforts and encouraged my clients to do the same. We all made efforts to connect with our existing client base to check in and see how they're doing. When we work together and lend a hand to support each other, we are stronger.

Still, I am convinced that a few good things have transpired in 2020. Video conferencing became commonplace, and that reduced most white-collar workers' need to travel for work. The air quality improved when fewer cars or planes were in operation. Many people pivoted and reinvented their careers. Others

THE GIVE TO GET PRINCIPLE

became strict with their budget and saved more money because their social obligations were put on hold for many months. More people got outside on their bicycles and skateboards while others learned TikTok dances and cleaned their closets. Humanity adjusted, and so did the earth. Yes, 2020 sucked in many ways, but it woke us up, too. For that, I am thankful.

The graphic you see above was a social media post from Gary Vaynerchuk, a social media leader I deeply respect. When I saw it, I made it a screensaver on my computer. I wanted to see it every day to remind myself how much I've pivoted and grown since facing the challenges of COVID-19 and the crumbling economy. He's right, you know. This year woke me up. It woke us all up. It's up to me to pick myself up, dust myself off, and keep making every effort to progress forward.

That is why I wrote this book for you. I wanted to share what we were doing to grow our businesses. I know that these practices work, regardless of what's going on in the economy. When we focus on our clients and do everything in our power to help them, inspire them, and lift them up, it's valuable. Relationship marketing is vital to your business's survival. Your relationships are the currency that will attract the other three currencies out there: Money, Time, and Knowledge.

CHAPTER 12
Thriving Beyond Surviving

Had I written this book sooner, I am convinced that more business owners would have thrived in 2020 and not just survive. But then, would they have listened?

When we get comfortable, we tend to stick with the things we know work for us. But when all hell breaks loose and we have fewer options, we figure out that we need to change things up quickly. If we don't, we risk losing more than we ever dreamt possible.

Carm Capriotto of Remarkable Results is a podcaster that caters to the auto repair industry. I was listening to an interview he had with Dr. David Weiman, a psychology professor, that outlined how a relaxed state will positively affect customer responses. When a connection is created between the client and the service provider, the clients rely on the service provider to help them. This positive connection creates experience and fosters trust. Showing kindness can be a Give To Get Principle that is often repaid in years of customer loyalty and referrals.

But let's look at an example. When an auto repair shop shows compassion and uses language with their client that uses simple terms and is easy to understand, the clients feel innate value in good feelings. Therefore, if a small business does what it can to

THE GIVE TO GET PRINCIPLE

help the customers and show kindness, the results will be loyal, happy customers.

Many workers know this but have not been able to articulate it. The pandemic has created chronic and acute stress for everyone in some measure. To add, every customer who comes to your business has a problem hoping you will help them solve. When they are not in a relaxed state, but rather a stressed state, what kind of response can you show? What are the various ways you can help them? If you can figure out a formula that your business can follow consistently, you are helping to reduce their stress and form a deeper, positive connection with them.

Creating a stress-free customer service experience and creating positive associations like a warm smile, friendly service, and kindness are the building blocks for a successful business. Strong connections build long-lasting relationships, which is a critical component in creating raving fans who share the good news about your business.

The secret to creating more revenue for your business is to keep building great relationships with more people, so your business grows positively correlated with your expanding network of clients. Master this, and you will be incredibly successful.

THE GIVE TO GET PRINCIPLE

CHAPTER 13
Together, We Are Stronger

It wasn't until the Corona Virus that I was able to LIVE the advice of Give To Get rather than tell other people's stories. I needed to experience these principles myself in my own business to support my clients who were panicked and desperate for my help. Instead of charging them extra and taking advantage of the situation, I wholeheartedly gave them a lot of additional support, marketing help, and love because we are all in this together. And together, we are stronger.

Emails and posts were shared when my clients and I all came together to pool our ideas. We shared, with permission, among our community, and everyone benefited. Everyone's businesses performed better, regardless of what state they lived/worked in.

After the first wave of shelter-in-place panic passed, my phone didn't ring within concerned calls as frequently, and that's okay. We got everyone through the first wave. Because we worked together, each client sprung into action and leaned into their marketing. Auto repair businesses are deemed essential businesses, and if they were shut down, it was for a relatively short time. Most people across the United States rely on their vehicles for transportation. As a result, the auto repair industry started to do better once we got into summer.

THE GIVE TO GET PRINCIPLE

Why were auto repair shops busy during the summer? The reason was because people were stuck inside their homes during the first few months of the pandemic, and were itching to get outside or go on road trips. RV sales and camper rentals skyrocketed! Americans love their freedom, after all. Having a reliable car gives people options to have a temporary escape, if only for a little while.

Two of my clients, Ernie Skillingstad of Ernie's Inc. in Olympia, WA, and Robert Henderson of Henderson's Line-Up in Grants Pass, OR, used the trending popularity of motorhome travel to their advantage. They each employed the Give To Get Principle in different ways.

At Ernie's Inc. in Olympia, WA, they repair all aspects of an RV or trailer. From the engine and brakes to the roof and plumbing, they fix it all. But their customer service experience also includes lessons on how to drive your Recreational Vehicle. Ernie's Inc. attracts many first-time coach owners who are intimidated by their RV, trailer, camper, or motorhome. The RV lifestyle is a great one, but it takes practice before you feel like a veteran RVer. Ernie and his team spend the extra time showing their customers how to back up and drive their trailers or coaches so they can feel safer and more confident. Clients will travel hundreds of miles to get to their RV repair shop because of their excellent work and customer service.

THE GIVE TO GET PRINCIPLE

Henderson's Line-Up in Grant's Pass, OR, is similar in that they also do RV repair. Their family business motto is "Providing Safer and Happier Driving for More People," and they've been serving the RV community since 1961. But they have another division of their business called SuperSteer, which are performance parts that help to stabilize the steering and drivability of RVs and trailers. SuperSteer Parts help motorhome drivers swerve to miss hitting something in the road but not lose control of their rig. Robert Henderson and his wife, Barbara, use the Give To Get Principle, too. Before COVID, they frequently attended RV Rallies across the country and hosted free RV Care Clinics and Inspections. Today, they continue to offer video tutorials, classes, and other educational programs that allow other RV repair shops to install their SuperSteer Parts. It's quite a successful business model! They have built a large fan base, and they are always grateful to God for allowing them to serve their community and help keep them safe.

The good news for both of these shops? Their businesses are doing very well and continue to grow. Both shops take great care of their employees -- who are often family members and longtime coworkers -- and their clients, who they treat like family. They have been leaning into their marketing and Give To Get philosophy. They have found plenty of good in a down economy, and I'm proud of their progress.

Quarter 4: Your Roadmap To Success

To get you and your team to level up in business, I have several action steps to give you the roadmap to success. I want to give you hope. I want to provide you with examples of proven strategies that will help you grow. Are you ready?

THE GIVE TO GET PRINCIPLE

CHAPTER 14
Action Step #1 – Start By Finding Your Why

The very first step is to look deep within the purpose of your business. Why is it here? Is it only to make money? I would bet that money is not the real reason your company began. Money is a result of a higher purpose.

If you started the business, something burning in your soul made you want to begin, right? What was it that made you take steps to begin?

- Was it because you hated your old job?
- Was it because you thought there was a better way of doing business?
- Was it because you always wanted to work in your industry since you were a kid?
- Was it because your parents or grandparents were in the business before you?

We all have our "why." We can all be doing the same job, but we have different reasons for doing it.

It reminds me of an old story about three bricklayers and the power of purpose. When the first bricklayer was asked, "What

THE GIVE TO GET PRINCIPLE

are you doing?", he responded with, "I'm a bricklayer. I'm working hard, laying bricks to feed my family." The second bricklayer replied, "I'm a builder. I'm building a wall." But the third bricklayer, the most productive of the three and the future leader of the group, when asked the question, "What are you doing?" replied with a gleam in his eye, "I'm a cathedral builder. I'm building a great cathedral to The Almighty."

There are no wrong answers with these three bricklayers. They each have a purpose, a why, and they are all correct in their responses. However, all businesses that clarify their purpose and share that "why" with their team tend to have more cohesive operations. Do you only want your employees motivated to work because they have bills to pay? Or, do you want the employees who have a grander vision that will better serve the business and the community?

It reminds me of what Lee Richter once said in her business coaching workshop about employees and their behaviors. She explained that we are "renting" our employees' behavior, and they have three jobs: 1) To reduce our stress, 2) To save us money, and 3) To make us money. If your employees are not doing those three jobs, you will not get full value out of their service.

It is up to you as the business owner to let your team know what the "why" is for your business. This will help them to align their purpose and responsibilities to further the company's goal and cause. It's a win-win-win for you, your team, your customers, your vendors, and your community when everyone knows what your business stands for.

THE GIVE TO GET PRINCIPLE

If you are unclear about your why, you will see that uncertainty has a domino effect on your business. But when you become focused and clear about your higher purpose and how your business will help you get there, you can then share that broader vision with your team. Together, you can join forces and bring that vision into reality. Isn't that a beautiful goal to achieve? The unified purpose is so powerful!

So, what is your why? What is your purpose? Please write it down so you can get it out of your head and onto paper. Once it is written out, you will have an easier time sharing it with your team.

Go ahead and write down right here what it is that gets you out of bed every day to go to work? I'll wait for you. :-)

What is my "why"? What drives me toward my higher purpose? (If you run out of space, go ahead and get a fresh piece of paper so you can write it all down, share it with your team, fold it up, and place it here between these pages, so you don't forget. Bonus points if you put a date on it because you may be surprised to find that in 10 years, your why has shifted a bit.)

Take this time to write down your thoughts. Go ahead. I'll wait. :-)

"But, Jen! I don't own a business yet. I'm just an employee. What about me?"

Ah! Don't worry, my friend. I didn't write this book just for business owners. I wrote it for you, too. ;-)

THE GIVE TO GET PRINCIPLE

If you are a contractor, an intern, an employee, a volunteer, or a helper, you have a "why" as well. We all do!

So here's what I'd like you to do. I want you to write down your "why" as well.

"But why, Jen? I don't have control over the business." While that may be correct, you have your purpose and what you do every day in service to others helps you reach that higher vision for yourself.

To give you an example, think about going into a restaurant. You are seated at your table, and you notice that your server puts a lot of care and thoughtfulness into her job. After observing her over the next hour while you dine, you can tell that she is passionate about providing an exceptional dining experience. How does that make you feel? It makes you want to return to that restaurant and get seated in her section again. You may even ask for her name so you can remember to include it in the five-star review you write about the restaurant. Her passion and extra effort make your customer service experience a happy memory, and you may want more of that in the future.

Now, let's look at the opposite scenario. You go to that same restaurant for the first time, and you are seated at your table. The server takes a long time to collect your drink order and even longer to write down your food order, and then that server gets it wrong. On top of that, he is checking his phone and doesn't

THE GIVE TO GET PRINCIPLE

notice you trying to get a napkin. He seems distracted, aloof, and unengaged. How does that make you feel? Does it make you want to return to that restaurant? Does that make you want to write a five-star review?

Okay, let's compare. It's the same restaurant, right? Two different servers. Two completely different customer service experiences.

Now, let me ask you. Which server seems to love the job more? The first one?

Next question: If you heard that a friend of yours was opening up a new restaurant and is looking for talented employees, which server would you recommend for the job? The first one?

That's what I thought. Okay, you're probably thinking, "But Jen, how does that affect me in my job?" Well, if you love what you do, you are likely in alignment with your "why." If you don't like your job and are often thinking about leaving it, you are still searching for a place that will allow you to live your "why." Whatever you focus on, the Law of Attraction says that you will get more of it. Therefore, if you focus on a purpose-driven life and do your best to find jobs aligned with your "why", you will achieve your goals faster.

I want you to write down your "why" right now.

What is my "why"? What drives me toward my higher purpose?

THE GIVE TO GET PRINCIPLE

(Go ahead and get a fresh piece of paper so you can write it all down. Then, share it with your team so you are all on track and you don't forget. Bonus points if you put a date on it because you may be surprised to find that in 10 years, your why has shifted a bit.)

CHAPTER 15
Action Step #2 – Discover The Superpower Of Yourself And Your Team

I am a big believer in playing towards individual strengths. If you ask a fish to climb a tree, for example, that fish will fail. But if you request that fish to swim, the fish is playing toward its natural gifts. That is the culture we foster here at Rock Star Marketing.

I love talking with clients, so, naturally, I handle the majority of sales and marketing. Jessie loves writing Search Engine Optimized content for web pages, so she gravitates toward those larger projects. Chris enjoys blog writing, so he's happy diving into those monthly blogs. Rene is our graphic design superhero, so he's in charge of our Media Division that produces graphics and video projects. Together, we are like the superheroes in Marvel or DC Comics. We all bring our talents to the collective, and we lift each other up as we play to our strengths.

When you discover the superpowers of each team member at your business, you will see many benefits. Therefore, I suggest you go on discovery and uncover who excels at various things in your company.

THE GIVE TO GET PRINCIPLE

You can either work in this book or take a separate sheet of paper for this assignment. I will provide you a list of questions, and I'd like you to discuss it with your entire team. The goal is to find out who enjoys working on various facets so you can have them serve in roles they would thrive in. Are you ready?

Okay, here we go!

- Who enjoys talking with customers?
- Who has a talent for working with numbers?
- Who likes to problem solve?
- Who has a knack for developing long-term relationships?
- Who loves their environment to be neat and tidy?
- Who enjoys cooking?
- Who enjoys throwing parties?
- Who loves to get into the technical details?
- Who has a designer's eye?
- Who always has the right words to say in a delicate situation?
- Who is the fastest to complete projects?
- Who is the most thorough and detailed individual?
- Who enjoys being on the go and moving around?
- Who does their best work at their desk?
- Who loves animals and would enjoy caring for the company mascot?
- Who has excellent taste in music?
- Who easily makes people laugh and breaks up the tension?
- Who is the creative one in the group?
- Who enjoys writing thank you notes?
- Who is the fastest typist?
- Who has the best handwriting?
- Who enjoys making desserts?

THE GIVE TO GET PRINCIPLE

- Who is the most likely to take everyone out for a drink?
- Who is the one most likely to know everyone in town?
- Who is a great spokesperson?
- Who is the one who can fix anything?
- Who is extremely passionate about personal growth and development?
- Who is the one you would confide in?
- Who takes outstanding notes?

If you ask your team these questions, I suspect you'll have a lot of fun discovering everyone's superpowers. If you have other items you would like to add to the list, please do so. Not only will each person play to their strengths, but they will also appreciate and cherish the talents of their teammates. Have fun with this exercise. :-)

CHAPTER 16
Action Step #3 – Pay Attention To Attitude

Let's do another exercise. I want you to review these questions and think deeply about your answers.

In general, what is your attitude when you are at work? I know we all can have atypical days where our mindset needs an adjustment. But for the most part, how would people describe your attitude?

What about the attitude of your teammates at work? What is the perspective of each individual?

Lastly, what is the attitude of the entire group? Are they excited about the work they're doing? Are they passionate about providing top-notch customer service? Are they rude, or worse?

I like to think that marketing is an attitude, not a department. Your attitude reflects the experience your customers can expect to receive. If you are getting a lot of mediocre to one-star customer reviews for your business, you may want to check your attitude and the attitude given off by your coworkers.

THE GIVE TO GET PRINCIPLE

When I see someone with a positive attitude, I see someone who is excited and happy about their work. If you really want to do something, no matter what it is, you can do it if you have the right attitude and are willing to put in some hard work. To add, if you are disciplined about your thoughts, finding the good in every situation, being positive, and getting rid of negative beliefs or attitudes, you will reach the next level of joyful fulfillment.

Got a bad attitude? People can see it and feel it.

Got a confident attitude? Guess what? People can see and feel that, too.

Your attitude is a direct correlation with your level of success. Victim mentality or a crappy attitude is like vomiting negativity onto someone else, and it doesn't feel good at all. A can-do attitude that leaves yourself and others feeling uplifted, inspired, and engaged is much better.

What is your attitude? What is the collective attitude within your business? If your attitude is anything less than favorable, you probably shouldn't expect to meet all your sales goals. But if you have a great attitude, chances are very high that you will succeed.

Remember the parable about the three bricklayers and the power of purpose? When each was asked, "What are you doing?" the attitude of the first bricklayer was, "I am doing my job so I can make money and feed my family."

THE GIVE TO GET PRINCIPLE

The second bricklayer had the attitude of, "I am building a wall."

However, the third bricklayer showed a great attitude by answering, "I am building a cathedral so the people will come inside and find God."

Though I'm sure we can all relate to the first and second bricklayers, the third bricklayer had an attitude that was not only positive but incredibly inspiring.

If you prefer a more modern parable, check out this meme I found on Reddit:

I work for McDonald's.

THE GIVE TO GET PRINCIPLE

Does your business culture foster a similar attitude to the third bricklayer or the third McDonald's employee? If not, you should try it on for size.

If the attitudes coming from your team are out of alignment with what your clients would like to see, your business could be facing big problems. When your team is happy, chances are greater that your clients will be pleased with their service.

If your business has a friendly, helpful, there's-no-problem-we-can't-solve attitude, your clients will be more attracted to you.

Conversely, if you have a defeated, grumpy, or negative attitude, your clients will be more likely to run the other way.

Write down answers to the following questions.

1. What is my current attitude, and could it be improved?

THE GIVE TO GET PRINCIPLE

2. What is the attitude of my team, and could it be improved?

3. Does my team's current attitude align with our company's mission and purpose?

CHAPTER 17
Action Step #4 – Define What You're Willing To Give To Get

Now that you have identified your why, superpowers, and attitude moving forward, let's define what you are willing to Give To Get.

It's nice to say you want to give, but if you don't have systems in place, how will you know it is being done consistently? Do you have a Customer Relationship Management software that tracks which customers received the gift and which ones have not?

I remember talking with shop owners Becki and Bryan McGinnis of Autovantage Service Center in Auburn, California, who wash every car that comes into their shop before returning the vehicle to the customer. That's a nice bonus for the customer. But what happens if they are short-staffed that day and cannot wash all of the cars? The customers who are accustomed to getting a free car wash are disappointed. So, whatever it is that you choose to give, make sure you do it consistently. Otherwise, your generous giving will become a liability when enough people see you failed to meet the expectations set in your customer reviews. Not fun, right?

Fortunately, this shop owner has a backup plan when he and his team cannot wash the cars before handing over the keys to the

THE GIVE TO GET PRINCIPLE

customers upon pickup. He gives them a voucher to the car wash that is less than a mile away. It is a great solution that keeps his clients happy, and the partnership with the car wash brings him new client referrals for auto repair. Pretty smart, huh?

Let's look at the many systems and processes you can use to help you track what has been given to your clients. Review this list and see how many of these systems and processes you have in place already.

Directions:
Rate yourself from 1 to 10 (with one meaning that you have nothing in place and 10 meaning that you're on top of your game). Next, I want you to tally up the total number and see where you are on a scale of 0 to 70.

Circle your lowest two scores and commit to improving this system and process.

Let's begin!

- CRM (Customer Relationship Management) software that fits your industry and allows you to document what you have done in the past with the client, what you plan to do at the next visit, and other reminders.   Score _____

- A Specials page on your website that offers discounts or limited-time offers for future repairs or services. Score_____

THE GIVE TO GET PRINCIPLE

- An email system that allows you to check-in with your client database, update them on what's new, offer valuable tips and tricks that could help them, and notify them of any events or special offers.   Score _____

- Tools like Infusionsoft or Clickfunnels, lead generation systems will help you capture prospects and place them into your database.   Score _____

- Phone lists that allow you to connect regularly for special needs and elderly clients who may not be technically savvy, and you want to check on their well-being.   Score _____

- Budget for giveaways that take place every month. You don't have to spend a lot on a mason jar filled with candy for Halloween if they can guess the correct amount of pieces inside that jar. You don't have to spend lots of money on a gift basket with some of your products inside. But you really should have a budget for anything you give away, so you don't break the bank.   Score _____

- Create a checklist that includes all of the Standard Operating Procedures. These SOPs define what you're willing to give away and how you will go about doing it.   Score _____

Total Score _____

Which two items have the lowest score that you will commit to improving? *(Write it down!)*

These systems and processes are the tips of the iceberg, but they should give you a good head start in helping you accomplish the Give To Get Principle.

THE GIVE TO GET PRINCIPLE

CHAPTER 18
Action Step #5 – Examples Of The Giveaways Other Businesses Use

For over a decade, I have been fortunate to interview hundreds of small businesses that share what they Give To Get. Everyone has a great story, and I confess that I fall in love with every single client I work with after hearing their stories. I can't help but admire their passion for exceptional customer service and making the world a better place through their time and talents.

So you can imagine how many of these thoughtful small businesses give away something that their clients can enjoy. Now before I share the list of my favorite giveaways, I want you to know that none of these freebies are expensive. Remember, when you create a positive, memorable customer service experience for your target audience, they are going to love you and share the good news about your business with everyone they know.

You want them to spread the good news about your business. Of course, you do! So, here are my 20 favorite giveaways, and I encourage you to dream up some of your own.

1. Your choice of a candy bar from five options.
2. A personal health kit -- complete with a facemask, hand sanitizer, and tissue paper.

THE GIVE TO GET PRINCIPLE

3. Small toys in a treasure chest.
4. A single rose.
5. Breath mints.
6. Cookies from a local bakery.
7. Hamburgers and hot dogs from the grill, made by the staff on Saturdays.
8. Art gallery openings with food trucks.
9. Snow cones.
10. Customer appreciation BBQ fundraiser with dog adoption.
11. A free used car to a lucky family in need.
12. A birthday cake for cars that reach 300K miles.
13. Loaner bicycles and dog leashes while you wait for your tires to be installed.
14. Free car care clinics.
15. A YouTube library of how-to videos.
16. A pad of sticky notes and a pen.
17. A smile.
18. Drawings for gift baskets on Mother's Day.
19. Loaner cars.
20. Pickup and delivery service.
21. Teaching new RV drivers how to maneuver and park their vehicles.

THE GIVE TO GET PRINCIPLE

What do you plan to give to your clients? How can you wow them and turn them into raving fans? Write down your ideas here and share these ideas with your team.

Idea #1:

Idea #2:

Idea #3:

THE GIVE TO GET PRINCIPLE

CHAPTER 19
Action Step #6 – Decide What You Can Give Freely Right Now

Not everyone has a large budget for giveaways. However, you and your team can take a good, solid look at your company values and decide together what you can give freely, right now.

- Is it a warm welcome and a smile?
- Do you remember their names? Can you ask how their vacation went? What about inquiring what's new with their parents, grandparents, or children?
- How about a ride home?
- If you like baking cookies, why not bake extras and share them with your clients?
- A handwritten thank you note goes a long way too.
- Do you have some bottled water in the refrigerator for a cold drink? How about a cup of coffee?
- A voucher, discount coupon, or a postcard celebrating your 1st anniversary is easy enough and inexpensive enough to print out, right?
- Or, better yet, send your clients a card on their birthdays.
- What about a carton of ice cream to share on a hot summer's day?
- Or maybe a free vacuum and car wash?
- Have you thought of a goodie bag for first time customers that includes several of the items listed above?
- Do you actively listen to your customers and enjoy heartfelt conversations with them when you make the time?

THE GIVE TO GET PRINCIPLE

Sometimes the only thing it costs is time. That extra value and care you provide will also justify your pricing. There are lots of low-cost options you can employ while giving to get.

However, here is a small warning. If you do all of these giveaways -- regardless of how much they cost -- and you are inconsistent about doing it, watch out. The customers will think that your high standards are slipping, and you increase the risk of them feeling like they didn't get their money's worth.

So, whatever you decide to give, be sure you and your team infuse it into your daily processes and procedures, so nothing gets skipped. Consistency is key.

In the last exercise, you wrote down three ideas about what you're willing to Give To Get. What are three more ideas that your team can come up with that they would be eager to give? Not only does this create buy-in with your team, but you may find they have some terrific ideas you wouldn't expect.

Are you ready for some fun? On the next page, let's have you jot down some terrific ideas!

Write down your team's ideas and discuss them with your team.

THE GIVE TO GET PRINCIPLE

Idea #1:

Idea #2:

Idea #3:

CHAPTER 20
Action Step #7 – Involve Your Team In Giving To Get

When you dream up all of these great ideas of giveaways to your clients, it is so important you get consensus and active participation from your team. When you recruit your co-workers to join you in giving to get, it will help ensure that your customers experience a consistent level of service.

If your team does not get actively involved in giving extra care and value to your clients, the customer service experience may appear inconsistent. For example, if one employee knows your vision of using the Give To Get Principle, that person may offer your client a ride to work or home. If your other employees are unaware of this option of a free ride, they may not provide it to the customer. When that same customer sees that one employee offers a ride, but the other one doesn't, that customer may favor working with the first employee who appears more thoughtful to the client's needs. Over time, the second employee may become envious because the first employee seems to have more positive reviews than the second employee. To fix this issue, make sure that all your employees understand that offering free rides is an option, and you may find that more team members are named in the positive customer reviews.

THE GIVE TO GET PRINCIPLE

Additionally, when your team is permitted to develop ideas on improving the customer service experience, they may find creative solutions that you didn't think about. Give them the power to make someone's day, and you will be delighted when they adopt the Give To Get Principle on their own to make your customer happy.

Here's a series of questions you can use to ensure all of your teammates are informed about what they can give to get. To do this exercise, get together with your team and write down the answers you create for each question:

What are the three things you consistently give to your clients?

When do you give those three things to your customers, and how frequently?

What happens when you are about to run out of those three things? Who replenishes those three things?

THE GIVE TO GET PRINCIPLE

If those three things are unavailable, what does your team suggest you give instead?

How can your team ensure these three things are given away consistently? What is the process they need to follow?

Do you offer your team regular opportunities to dream up new things to give away to your clients? How do these ideas get implemented?

THE GIVE TO GET PRINCIPLE

CHAPTER 21
Action Step #8 – Track And Measure Your Progress

Now that you know what you plan to give and your team is involved, the next step is to track and measure your progress. Here are some ideas to get you started, but feel free to add more metrics that best suit your style.

But to do this next exercise, you'll want to ponder these questions and enter the ones you want to use in a spreadsheet and/or some kind of tracking software. When you track and measure based on these questions, you can more easily collect accurate data from everyone involved.

1. What are you giving away?
2. How many of these items are given in one day? One week? One month? One quarter? One year?
3. How many people who received these items commented on it positively? In-person? On your social media channels? In a customer review? In an email or text message?
4. How many people who received these items commented on it negatively?
5. How much did you spend on these items?

THE GIVE TO GET PRINCIPLE

6. How many sales did you make because you gave away these items?

7. How many of these items were given away by each team member?

8. Who gave the most away, and why? Who gave the least away, and why?

9. Did these giveaways pay for themselves? If yes, how long did it take to see a return on investment?

10. Can you survey your clients and find out that of the various items you gave away, which one did they like or appreciate the most?

11. What other feedback are you getting about these items you are giving away? Comments about quality? Color? Size? Function?

12. If you could no longer give the popular items away, what would be a suitable replacement? Would the replacement cost more or less?

Be sure to instruct your team too. If you cannot measure or track your giveaways, it's harder to manage the results and make a profit. The goal is to track your giveaways in such a manner that you can visually assess monthly, quarterly, and annual performance patterns.

CHAPTER 22
Action Step #9 – Building Community

Now that your team has mastered giving, measuring, and tracking to your clients, pat yourself on the back. You've done great work so far.

Are you ready for the next level of the Give To Get Principle? The next step is to build a community around your business and show your community how you care for and support them.

An auto repair shop owner who does this beautifully is Brent Kniesel of Kniesel's Auto Service Centers. Brent and his family have three shops in Citrus Heights, Roseville, and Sacramento, California. They sincerely care for their local community, but they also spend a lot of time, effort, and money to make life better for underprivileged communities in other countries. Brent and his team want to impact the world, and they're doing it in numerous ways.

One of their newer projects involves local schools. Brent wants to dedicate 6% of the proceeds from each auto repair and gift it to a few local schools. To bring this Give To Get Principle to a real-life campaign, he contacted the San Juan School District to see if they would be open to Kniesel's Auto Service Centers doing some charity fundraising. He was contacted by the Family

THE GIVE TO GET PRINCIPLE

& Community Engagement Department and agreed to partner with the school district to donate books for a literacy campaign. Not only will Kniesel's Auto Service Centers be supplying books to the three schools closest to his three shops, but he'll also be creating branded bookmarks that will be given out with each book. He also plans to participate in a program that supports foster kids in these schools, making sure they have what they need to succeed in school. Lastly, he intends to continue working with the automotive technology class at San Juan High School, donating equipment and time to the kids interested in automotive careers.

Do you see the beauty in what Brent is doing by serving his community? Not only does he feel good about supporting others, but the larger community gets to see first hand how great the Kniesel Auto Service Centers brand is. Plus, those kids who grow up with donated books, bookmarks, school supplies, and automotive equipment will eventually grow up to drive cars of their own. His generosity helps the next generation of car owners become familiar with Kniesel's brand and perpetuate their family business's success. Brent is creating a win for his company, for the families he is serving, the schools he is partnering with, and a win for the community.

So, what are you willing to do for your community? I will list a few suggestions, and you can come up with some of your own, too:

- Sponsor a stretch of road and volunteer to pick up trash for a cleaner roadway.

THE GIVE TO GET PRINCIPLE

- Give away a donated vehicle to a disabled veteran or a family with a special needs child.
- Work with your favorite church or Rotary Club to see how your business can support their charities.
- Create an event that will bring the community together, like an art gallery opening in your lobby, plus one or two food trucks.
- Sponsor a local sports team or STEM program.
- Participate in Toys For Tots during the holiday season or Food Drives for your local food bank year-round.
- Host a blood drive to support your local Red Cross.
- Partner with other businesses to supply food to hungry families who can't find work or are homeless.
- Volunteer your team and time to help build a Habitat for Humanity home.
- Partner up with the vocational program in a nearby prison to give released prisoners a chance at earning an honest living.

There are so many things you can do to support your community. What ideas can you and your team come up with that get you excited about giving time and energy to make the world a better place? Go ahead. Write your ideas down, then discuss them with your team to make your dreams a reality.

Idea #1 is…

THE GIVE TO GET PRINCIPLE

Idea #2 is…

Idea #3 is...

THE GIVE TO GET PRINCIPLE

CHAPTER 23
Action Step #10 -- Mentor Others In Abundance Mentality

After you have mastered the Give To Get Principle, I invite you to take it to the next level: Mentor others in abundance mentality.

Joe Sevart, the owner of I-70 Auto Repair in Kansas City, was a tremendous mentor for me in this department. He is a very successful -- now retired -- shop owner who believes in abundance mentality. The more he gives, shares, and supports others, the more reciprocity he attracts. When we started working together in 2017, he told me that he believed that my marketing efforts made a huge difference in his business. His goal was to introduce me to the other members of his mastermind group so they, too, could benefit from my services.

Joe put the wheels in motion for me by sharing what I had to offer with everyone in his inner circle. He introduced me to his group members and his business coach. Once his coach, John Wafler, vetted me and offered advice about getting myself ready for the floodgates of work to open, I did everything I could to prepare myself. I knew their mentoring would bring a fountain of opportunity that would change my life and my marketing agency's path. Because Joe and John agreed to introduce me to

THE GIVE TO GET PRINCIPLE

their shop owners' extensive network, I would meet at least 120 shop owners and work with 50% of them over the next few years.

I tell this story because Joe Sevart and John Wafler are dyed-in-the-wool mentors who want to help other auto shop owners thrive. Joe and John are generous with their time, helping business owners take the next steps towards success. And they don't just do this for people like me. They also invite others into their inner circle to bring skills and services to help the whole mastermind group level up.

If you mentor others in abundance mentality, there are many opportunities to share your wisdom. If you are good at training and attracting new employees, share that knowledge. If you are a whiz at providing excellent customer service, share your wisdom. Don't worry about the competition taking your expertise and competing against you. Focus on giving the best possible customer service experience, and you'll be light years ahead of your competition.

When I started teaching my marketing classes to the auto repair industry, I shared my knowledge without hesitation. Several times, competitors of mine attended my classes. But I wasn't worried. I have owned my marketing agency since 2009, and I have built a career out of the knowledge I have accumulated. But I am always studying new marketing aspects, and I never stop reading business books, watching TED talks about marketing, and taking classes about the latest marketing trends. When

THE GIVE TO GET PRINCIPLE

I study hard to stay abreast of the changes in the marketing industry, I can share that knowledge without hesitation. Why? Because there is only one person on this planet with my unique perspective, and that one person is me. Those who want to work with me will find me, and those looking for a different style or approach will find the marketing agency that suits them best.

Taking an example of the ice cream shop, I can look at the freezer case and see 30 different flavors. I tend to favor one or two flavors, but occasionally I will try something new. Not everyone is going to like your favorite flavors, so that they will choose their own. I'm getting at this because I am an acquired taste, and those that like my style will choose me. If I'm not your favorite flavor, that's okay. There are other flavors out there that will better suit your tastes. Abundance mentality helps me stay calm in a competitive marketplace because I know that I attract my perfect clients. Because of the relationships we build, they will choose my flavor repeatedly for many years to come.

Today, I am mentoring others by sharing my marketing wisdom with business owners in many different industries. I know that many of these business owners are just getting started and don't have the budget to work with my marketing agency right now. But when I share information and help support them, I know they will remember me and call on me when their timing is right. I love offering a hand to others, so they know they are not on this path alone. I give my time and knowledge because I know it will come back to me, someday, somehow.

THE GIVE TO GET PRINCIPLE

Write down your answers to these questions:

- What can you do to mentor others?
- What do you want to do?
- Can you create an online course?
- Can you become a coach?
- Can you volunteer in a group and teach others what you know?

Ponder these questions and give yourself time to reflect. When you are ready, develop a plan about how you will mentor your employees, clients, vendors, community, and industry.

Mentoring others is rewarding. It's like taking one candle and using that candle to light all the other candles in the room. The one candle loses nothing when it lights others up. The one candle helps light up the entire room! Isn't that cool?

Plus, when you teach, you become a better student and learn from the experience. The more you take on a teaching role, the mastery of your subject will increase. When you serve as a mentor, you will grow to love seeing your students succeed and teach you new insights along the way.

What are you willing to do to light up everyone you touch?

THE GIVE TO GET PRINCIPLE

CHAPTER 24
Action Step #11 -- Ideas For Other Industries

For anyone who is not part of the auto repair industry, but you have stuck with me this far in the book, I have something just for you! Indeed, marketing is marketing, and the same ideas can apply to any business. However, I want to offer more Give To Get ideas for other industries.

My marketing agency specializes in the auto repair industry, yes, but we also work with many different industries. So, let's put on our thinking caps and create some great ideas on what you can give away for other business types.

Trades and Services

If you are in the roofing, construction, house painting, plumbing, electrical, welding, or home repair industries, I have some ideas for you.

In the blue-collar trades, we know that time is money, right? There aren't many plumbers or electricians who give away things for free. But it's all about the higher level of service that you can offer that fits well into the Give To Get Principle.

The number one suggestion I have for you is to refine the systems

THE GIVE TO GET PRINCIPLE

and processes you use to make a stress-free experience for your clients, your team, and your vendors.

I want to share a few examples so you can see what other businesses are doing that's working out very well and increasing their bottom line.

Scott Siemer of Just Leaks owns a commercial roofing company in San Jose, CA. He only works on flat, industrial roofs, and he has become a leader in the industry in three ways:

1. He offers roofing inspections that include full reports with photos. These comprehensive reports demonstrate to the client what shape the roof is in, if there is any water pooling up there, any risk of leaks, and any recommendations for energy-saving solar panels or cool roof systems. These free reports are incredibly detailed and thorough, providing their customers with a clear understanding of a roof's present condition and expected performance.

2. He also is an avid fan of vintage Ford Falcon station wagons, and he has a fleet of them. He has converted these classic gas-powered vehicles into electric vehicles to show how dedicated he is to energy-saving tactics. Their Ford Falcons are eye-catching and help this roofing company stand apart from other roofing companies.

THE GIVE TO GET PRINCIPLE

3. Scott also believes that taking great care of his team is extremely important to stay healthy and productive. That is why Just Leaks provides a healthy bagged lunch to every employee so they can eat healthy, not have to worry about leaving the job site to hit a restaurant, and save money, too.

Nico Basurto of Basurto Painting in San Jose, CA, owns a painting company that serves residential and commercial properties. The majority of his clients are single-family homeowners, but he does substantial painting projects for apartments, commercial buildings, and rentals.

1. He has a great story that shares his "why," so he has produced a small pamphlet that tells about his experience, shows photos of his work, and outlines what his clients can expect when working with his team.

2. He loves to educate his clients on the painting process and advises them on the project scope through his vast experience. Because of his guiding nature, he has earned the trust of many homeowners and real estate professionals who feel he is the best in the business.

3. Nico is a perfectionist, and he wants his clients to be thrilled with their quality. He makes it a policy to have neat and tidy work vehicles, and his team members are required to clean up after themselves on every project,

so they leave it better than they found it. Before a project is declared complete, he does a walkthrough with his clients to assess the work so he can immediately address any errors or imperfection. As a result, his clients are thrilled with his team's work, and they are happy to refer him to others.

Do you see how both Scott and Nico use the Give To Get Principle in their business? They have a generous nature that allows their clients to trust them. They give away time so they can educate others about the nature of their work. In return, their clients and their team give them their trust. It's a beautiful win-win for everyone involved.

Medical Services

Suppose you are in the medical, dental, med-spa, plastic surgery, ophthalmology, nutrition, chiropractic, veterinary clinics, or other health fields. In that case, there are several ideas you can use as well.

Again, in the medical profession, you don't often see people giving services away for free. But I would argue that a higher level of service allows your target audience to feel that you are giving them extra value and care. Here are some examples that I have seen with my clients in the health industry:

Dr. Patricia Van Kooten of Lighthouse Family Dentistry in Monterey, CA, wants to make a dental visit as pleasant as possible.

THE GIVE TO GET PRINCIPLE

That is why she has a garden view in each room of her office. She speaks in a soft voice, and her mannerisms are very gentle. Soft music plays over the sound system. If the temperature is a little chilly, she offers a nice, fluffy blanket to you so you can stay toasty warm. Because Dr. Van Kooten wants to reduce the risk of COVID spreading to her staff or patients, she installed the AERIS air purification system in her office. The technology of the Swiss-made "Aeris Air 4" air purifier is impressive, for it sucks in the air and removes particles with 99.995% efficiency. Proprietary Zinc Mineral and Silver Ion technology incorporated into the filters and housing will kill and disintegrate microbes. The air purification system and the relaxing environment she creates has earned her rave reviews and has made her one of the leading dentists on the Monterey Peninsula.

Dr. Paul Dougherty of Dougherty Laser Vision in Southern California is known as "the Doctor's Doctor" and has earned himself the reputation of being the Lasik surgeon of the Hollywood stars. He is a leader in his field, for sure, but his Give To Get Principle is witnessed through his Andrew Dougherty Foundation. Every year, Dr. Dougherty donates his time and talent to a developing country whose citizens need eye surgery. For example, he went to Haiti to offer free cataract surgery for anyone who could meet with him throughout his "5 Day Mission". He's had people walk great distances and stand in line as he worked back to back on patients who would have gone blind if it were not for his generous efforts. Through his charitable giving, he is helping disadvantaged people from around the world see clearly again.

THE GIVE TO GET PRINCIPLE

Dr. Van Kooten and Dr. Dougherty are both using the Give To Get Principle to provide comfort in a situation where many patients feel stressed out. They do their part to give extra comfort and care so those that they serve feel safe, cared for, and valued. Again, their small-scale and large-scale generosity creates a win-win situation for their patients, their reputation, and for humanity.

Professional Services

Law firms, accounting services, temp agencies, Human Resource consultants, business coaches, marketing agencies, engineering firms, real estate agents, and other professional services can also add a lot of extra value and care to create reciprocity.

1. Offer a free consulting session for a limited time, like 15-30 minutes. You will share knowledge, and the prospect will learn what you do so they can decide to work with you.

2. Touch upon the five senses when prospects and customers visit your place of business. What can you provide that allows them to see, hear, touch, taste, and smell the benefits of what you're offering? Using real estate as an example, I've visited successful open houses that have had soft lighting accents placed throughout the house (see), music playing in the background (hear), cookies in the oven (taste), scented candles (smell), and a friendly handshake (touch). The result? A home with multiple offers that quickly sells.

THE GIVE TO GET PRINCIPLE

3. Host a free webinar that educates people on things they need to know if they want to be successful. If they learn from you but aren't ready to work with you yet, that's okay. What you're doing is planting a seed that will grow into a future client.

Here's an exercise for any business in the service industry with a commercial office: Define how you can touch all five senses in your business.
1. If you have a popcorn machine in your lobby, you capture the senses of smell and taste.
2. If you place art that represents your industry, plus graphs that show positive results, you appeal to the importance of sight by showing both beauty and logic.
3. If you offer salt scrub in the washroom for when people wash their hands, cloth towels, and high-quality hand lotion, you capture touch and smell.
4. When you play soft music or play a demonstration video on a monitor in your lobby, you appeal to both hearing and sight.

You can decide what makes the most sense for your business.

Caring Services

Child care, elder care, pet care, rehabilitation, and mental health care all have something in common. They all require a certain level of trust, patience, love, support, and anticipating other people's needs.

THE GIVE TO GET PRINCIPLE

1. Provide healthy, organic snacks and meals to those in your care.
2. Host a webinar that educates people on the processes you use to care for those you serve.
3. Make a video showing the correct techniques of transferring a disabled person from a wheelchair to a bed.
4. Create a blog article or video about five things people should know about your field of expertise.
5. Start or join a professional association and serve as a mentor to others.
6. Educate others on how they can help care for those with special needs.

Food and Beverage Industries

Wineries, restaurants, bakeries, grocery stores, coffee houses, culinary schools, restaurant suppliers, produce brokers, farmers, and fishers can use the Give To Get Principle as well. This industry is the one that is most widely recognized for free samples, which always creates a return on investment.

It's easy to list some of the things this industry regularly does:

1. Free product samples at Costco or other markets
2. Ice cream samples at your favorite local shop
3. Free dessert on your birthday
4. Free appetizer for loyal customers

THE GIVE TO GET PRINCIPLE

5. Taste samples in the wine tasting room
6. Passing out slices of fresh fruit at the Farmer's Market
7. Handing out small bites of the meal you prepared as a demonstration at the grocery store

Fitness Industry

Personal trainers, dance studios, coaches, physical therapists, marathon organizers, ballroom dance instructors, golf pros, and others in the fitness industry have a lot they can give. Here are some of the most popular methods of Giving To Get in this field:

1. Make a video showing the proper technique people should know about.
2. Create a video of an interview sharing why you love what you do and why you're doing it.
3. Share success stories and client breakthroughs.
4. Post a video of you doing what you do best so people can see you in action.
5. Create a behind-the-scenes video so you can educate everyone about what you have to do before the big competition.
6. Document your progress in a blog or video so you can give others hope about reaching their goals.

Hospitality & Travel Industry

Airlines, hotels, transportation agencies, event planners, entertainers, and support services can also use the Give To Get Principle:

THE GIVE TO GET PRINCIPLE

1. Offer free snacks and beverages on a flight.
2. Hand out warm cookies when guests check into your hotel.
3. Send a file with your music so the bride and groom can listen and see if they like your band's sound.
4. Educate your clients on how to host a memorable bar or bat mitzvah on a budget.
5. Hold a contest and give away useful or memorable prizes with your logo on them.
6. Allow the opportunity for a discount on spa services for frequent visitors.
7. Show the hotel owners that you're serving that you have a solution to their problem, and you'll do the first proof of concept for free so they can try it before they commit to your contract.
8. Give your guests a free ride to the airport.
9. Welcome first-timers with a glass of wine or beer.
10. Escort your guests to their room and offer to turn on the suite's fireplace for them.
11. If there is a problem related to customer service, give your team the power to turn that frown upside down.
12. Reward your team when they receive good customer reviews.

Do you see how easy it is to develop ideas that will create raving fans for your business? I love coming up with ideas, and I hope you do, too. When we give our best, the people we serve will appreciate our efforts and give us their loyalty and repeat business in return.

THE GIVE TO GET PRINCIPLE

Now, I was hoping you could write down three things you can do in your business that will allow you to use the Give To Get Principle.

Idea #1 is…

Idea #2 is…

Idea #3 is...

Once you decide which ideas you want to pursue, be sure to inform your team, track and measure your progress, adjust as needed, and mentor others so they can become successful, too.

THE GIVE TO GET PRINCIPLE

The Give To Get Principle formula in a nutshell:
1. Create an idea.
2. Share with your team.
3. Execute your idea.
4. Track & Measure your progress.
5. Rinse and Repeat.
6. Mentor others by sharing what you've learned.

THE GIVE TO GET PRINCIPLE

CHAPTER 25
Are You Willing?

I hope you found my deep dive into the Give To Get Principle helpful. What I shared with you is simple to execute. And because you are already on your path to success in your business, it is very likely you already knew so many things we discussed. However, I feel confident that even if you are very familiar with this idea of reciprocity, there are a few golden nuggets here that will allow you to take your customer service experience to the next level. If you want to develop a full Tribe of raving fans, the stories I've shared should get you well on your way towards that goal.

But before we finish, I have a few questions for you.

What are you willing to do to develop a client database of happy customers who are eager to share the good news about your team and refer new clients to your business?

- Are you willing to do the work to get what you want?
- Is your team willing to put in the effort to help you get there?
- What obstacles need to be moved out of the way for you to achieve your goals?

If you know the answers to these questions, and you have a plan on how to reach your desired level of success, that's fantastic!

THE GIVE TO GET PRINCIPLE

You've got a plan of action, and you know that you will attract a loyal following step-by-step.

If you still feel overwhelmed by all the steps you need to take, may I make a recommendation?

If you need further help after reading this book, I encourage you to contact me directly. I am happy to meet with you and discover what issues you face, learn about your business, find out what will happen if you don't improve your situation, and provide some ideas on how we can turn things around. I want you to know that you are not alone and that my Rock Star Squad is here to support you.

Is that something that you want to get started with? If yes, contact me right away at www.rock-star-mktg.com/discovery and fill out the request for a Discovery Session. It's free, it won't take long, and it's a great way to make a new friend. :-)

I look forward to hearing from you. I do this because I love helping other small business owners, and I want to see you and your business thrive. I am your sister in support, and it will be an honor serving as one of your cheerleaders!

To your success!

Jennifer Filzen
Your Favorite Rock Star Marketer

As a result of our marketing agency's efforts, team, attitude, and skills, Rock Star Marketing has helped over 700 small businesses grow their client base and reach their goals of earning their next million dollars in revenue. We do this by using The Give To Get Principle and telling the stories of our clients in such a way that it touches the hearts and minds of their ideal customers. We are looking for small business owners who want to take their business to the next level. Who do you know that could benefit from what Jennifer Filzen and the Rock Star Marketing Squad can provide? If you or anyone else could prosper from working with our marketing agency, contact Jennifer Filzen today.

Email: jennifer@rock-star-mktg.com
Phone: 408-833-9868
Monterey, California

Connect with Jennifer Filzen online:
www.rock-star-mktg.com
www.jenniferfilzen.com
www.wcsdanceco.com

Facebook: https://www.facebook.com/jennifer.filzen/
Twitter: https://twitter.com/RockStarMRY
Instagram: https://www.instagram.com/jenniferfilzen/
LinkedIn: https://www.linkedin.com/in/jenniferfilzen/
YouTube: https://www.youtube.com/user/jenfilzen

www.ingramcontent.com/pod-product-compliance
Lightning Source LLC
Chambersburg PA
CBHW070644220526
45466CB00001B/289